WORDS ARE STONES

CARLO LEVI

WORDS ARE STONES

Impressions of Sicily

Translated from the Italian by
Angus Davidson

FARRAR, STRAUS & CUDAHY
NEW YORK

First Printing, 1958

Copyright © 1951, 1958 by Farrar, Straus & Cudahy, Inc.

Library of Congress catalog card number: 58–10512

Words are Stones is a translation of Carlo Levi's
Le parole sono pietre. The section of this book
describing the visit of former mayor of New York
Vincent Impellitteri to his birthplace was first
published in *The Reporter*.

Manufactured in the United States of America
by H. Wolff, New York

Designed by Marshall Lee

WORDS ARE STONES

Introduction

The writings which are collected in this volume
belong to different periods: Parts I and II go back to
1951 and 1952, and were published at the time; Part
III, on the other hand, belongs to July and August
of the year 1955, and has never been published.

It has so happened that circumstances and a variety
of interests have, in recent times, encouraged me to
write a number of articles and essays, descriptions
and reports of journeys in Italy; and my publishers
felt that it would not be inopportune to bring them
together into a single book. The first suggestion they
made to me was that they should *all* be reprinted,
regardless of the fragmentary character—like that of
anthology—which would result from such an arrange-
ment, since doubtless a kind of connecting link would
become apparent, a unity not merely of style and of
vision but also of subject: for all these writings,
whether they were concerned with the South or the
North, with the peasant risings or the floods in the

Po delta, with the pastoral world of Sardinia or the lesser known happenings of the Partisan period, focused attention upon places and people in Italy at particular moments in their own history, in particular situations, all of them intimately connected with the acquisition of a new consciousness, with a self-assertion that was showing itself for the first time, with a first and never-to-be-repeated awakening to life.

Subsequently it seemed more advisable to limit the subject of the book to a more restricted space and time, and to publish at present only those writings that deal with the Sicily of recent years, thus forming a small book which would be not only slimmer and lighter but at the same time more homogeneous and more compact, leaving till later the possible publication of the remainder.

The present book, therefore, was not conceived originally with a narrative structure of its own, nor did it arise out of any preordained scheme or any single, fundamental intuition. The reader must not expect to find in it, as in *Christ stopped at Eboli* a first discovery of a dawning world and of its dimensions and of the bond of love that alone makes knowledge of that world possible; nor must he expect to find, as in *The Watch,* a complex and entirely frank picture of a decisive turn in the history of all men and of every man, and, at the same time, of the sense of time's infinite contemporaneity. Let him seek rather for simpler and more modest things, for an account of three journeys to Sicily and of how matters there strike the heedful eye of a traveler without prejudices. If by chance he finds something more, let him welcome it as a good bargain.

And now I think it desirable to add a few notes, which may perhaps interest the reader when he has finished the book.

The first sketch, describing the return of the mayor of New York to his native village, together with his "nativity" and "epiphany," was published immediately after the event, in the autumn of 1951, not only in *Illustrazione Italiana*—in which the other writings in Part I of this volume appeared too—but also in an American magazine, *The Reporter.* As can be seen from the text, there was no satirical intention in the mind of the author, but it was quite possible for a malicious reader to try and apply such an interpretation, and the American translation—deliberately, perhaps—gave a certain emphasis to those parts of the article which, to a reader of this kind, might have appeared ironical. However, what might perhaps have proved displeasing to a public figure less "natural" than "Mr. Impy," was, to the mayor, by no means so: he ordered a hundred copies of the magazine to distribute among his friends, and thanked the editor (who was perhaps not altogether innocent) with real emotion.

The miners' strike at Lercara Friddi, of which a moment of the first phase is here described, continued for some time longer and ended in complete success for them; Signor Ferrara, the owner of the mines (who is here called "N.," from Nerone or Nero, the nickname by which he was known in the district), was forced, contrary to all his expectations, to come to terms and to surrender. This was the beginning of his downfall. The miners' movement, which was born at that moment, with that first victory, has had its ups and downs during these last years, its times of expansion and its times of depression; but it had made a start and it did not turn back. Ferrara, however, after the first defeat, lost the prestige upon which alone his power was founded, and never recovered his position. A charge was brought against four of his inspector-slave drivers, who were accused of ill-treating his employees working in the mine, and they were found guilty and condemned. As a result of this unexpected occurrence Signor Ferrara (who had managed, somehow or other, to escape being incriminated in company with his dependents, who were acting under his orders) was expelled from the Christian-Democratic Party, of which he was the chief exponent in the district; and his star began to decline. But when I wrote and published this account, he was still in the full flower of his strength, as the following tale shows.

A few weeks after my visit to Lercara, there arrived there, with his paintbox and easel, a young artist from Cesena who intended to stay here some time in order to do studies from the life for a picture of miners. He had arrived at Lercara by chance, without any knowledge of the situation there, merely because those particular sulphur mines had been indicated to him as being the most favorable for his work, and perhaps also because they are the first to be met with as you come from Palermo. He did not know Sicily and the South, and everything appeared novel and interesting to him. He was a tall, fair young man (I got to know him when he came to see me soon afterward and told me of his adventures), gentle and mild in character, but at the same time obstinate when he had come to a decision, and with a sort of serene courage. No sooner, therefore, had he arrived at Lercara and installed himself in a room than he presented himself to Signor Ferrara and asked for a permit to go down the mine and draw and paint the miners at work. Signor Ferrara, using the same ambiguous methods as I had already experienced from him said neither yes nor no: he would ask the opinion of the engineers and technicians, and so on: in short, he kept him dangling for several days. The painter began to be aware of the situation at Lercara and realized he was not welcome there, but he stayed on and continued to press his request. The atmosphere around him grew more and more hostile, until it became positively provocative. As he went through the streets, members of the Mafia, crouching against the walls like lizards, their hands in their trouser belts, looked him up and down with fixed, snakelike eyes and spat on his shoes. Staying at Lercara began to be extremely uncomfortable, but he refused to own himself defeated. But, since there is just one mine there which does not belong to Ferrara, he decided, when he discovered this, that he would go and paint there; so off he started with his brushes and other implements. His way took him through a deserted countryside, and, at a bend, he saw an old man sitting on a stone at the side of the road, cutting slices from a big hunk of bread with a long, sharp, pointed knife. As he came up to him the old man, without rising or moving turned the point of the knife toward him, with an almost imperceptible gesture, and without raising his voice, said: "No one goes past here." And, in truth, no one was going past. The young painter realized who it was who had sent this underling to bar his way; and, with his youthful sense of justice, he was indignant, upbraiding the old man bitterly and asking him if he was not ashamed of the job he was doing. This left the old man untroubled and unmoved. He held up the piece of bread and said: "This bread is stale, but it's good."

Since painting was impossible, the young artist made up his mind to be satisfied with taking some photographs of miners as they came out of the sulphur mine, to be used later as documents for his paintings; and so, one day, with camera and tripod, he placed himself at the edge of the road in front of the mine, at a time when the workmen who had finished their shift were coming out. While he was intent on adjusting his sights, a car came suddenly up behind him at great speed and made straight for him; it actually grazed him on one side and he had barely time to throw himself into the ditch. The car continued on its way and stopped with a sharp jamming on of brakes in the midst of the workmen who were coming

8

out. The young painter picked himself up and ran toward the car, protesting at what had happened. He recognized the man at the wheel as one of Signor Ferrara's sons, who started to laugh at his protests and said to him: "I might easily have run you over. This is just a warning; another time you won't get off so lightly. Here, in this place, I can run you over whenever I like, because this is *my* place, and we've made it clear to you in all sorts of ways that you're not welcome and that you'd better go away."

The young man, who had an obstinate faith in justice, considered it his duty to report the matter to the police. Accompanied by a few miners, who had been witnesses of the incident, he went to the police station and asked to see the superintendent. He was told he was not there. He was pertinacious and determined, however; he did not leave the anteroom, but waited for several hours. When after six hours the superintendent grew tired of being besieged in this way and decided to receive him, he listened to his tale and then told him that, for his own good, he refused to receive his report; he certainly did not realize, he said, either where he was nor with whom he had to deal; he was young and a stranger, and he must not ask *him*, the superintendent—who would anyhow never agree to it—to expose him to grave dangers the seriousness of which he obviously did not appreciate; his report, in fact, would not be accepted, in spite of his persistence. It was only then that the painter from Cesena made up his mind to close his paintbox and fold up his easel and take his departure.

With regard to Bronte and the duchy, the situation, as far as I can make out, has not changed substantially during these last years, in spite of a scheme for a partial breaking up of the estate, affecting about 10,000 acres—a scheme not yet realized, and goodness knows when it will be—and a repetition of the peasant agitations. After my article had been published I received an extremely kind personal letter from the duke of Bronte inviting me as a guest to his "manor house," the Castello di Maniaci, and saying he was sure that a sincere exchange of views between us might be of real benefit to the condition of the impoverished peasants of the region. I accepted his invitation with great pleasure, but alas, various circumstances independent of my own wishes have so far prevented me from going back to the straw-stacks of the duchy.

The problem there is the problem of reform, of the land, of the real possession of the land, of its political possession—there, as in the whole of the South. My journey to Bronte, and round Mount Etna, and to Aci Trezza, had a positive result at the time, in 1952: I recrossed the Straits and, before returning to Rome, stopped in the country districts of Calabria to see for myself how the reform was working there, and what changes the small amount of land reform that had been realized had effected in the lives and thoughts of the peasants. I then wrote and published a long description of this journey, which was intended, in my original plan of this book, to find a place in it, together with all the other things I had written on various country districts of Italy and the happenings there. In my article this journey was shown as having taken place in company with the same foreign lady that I had met in the Malavoglia country (she was a little different here, however, being interested in social problems and the struggle against illiteracy), and with an agrarian expert, originator of the first inquiries into the question of land reform and its first applications, which he proceeded gradually to explain to us, during the journey, with the abstract enthusiasm of the "practical" idealist. As usual, it was a very rapid journey, lasting only two days; but we encountered an infinite number of human beings and of varying conditions which, as they piled up on top of each other and jostled together in one's memory, formed a picture of an unstable world, a world in suspense, and of the point of all-embracing crisis at which the operation of land reform had arrived. From Paola, gateway of the Sila Mountains and of the remote estates of the marquisate, we went on up to Cosenza, which was seething like a military headquarters. We left it again for the plateau, stopping everywhere to look and to ask questions, among mistrustful, puzzled *contadini* and officials who seemed to pop up from everywhere, like mushrooms after rain, zealous crusaders in an abstract battle. At San Giovanni in Fiore we went to the land reform organization center and talked with some wan-looking reticent *assegnatari;** and at the labor exchange, in an

* Peasants to whom portions of land have been assigned under the land reform distribution scheme.

11

atmosphere warm with protests and flashing glances among black cloaks, we listened to peasant poems condemning the methods of the land reform:

> *Si si benuto cu la leggi a mmanu*
> *U meritu e chi neri lu sapimo:*
> *I muorti e li feriti re Melissa*
> *E lutte camu fattu e chi facimu.*†

We pursued our way through the deserted lands of the barons and the brigands, stopping at the houses of the first *assegnatari,* and in the evening were caught in a downpour of rain at Santa Severina, high upon its rock. We fled from thence and stopped for the night at Crotone, in the warm air of the Ionian Sea; and our journey began again next morning, taking us to Isola Capo Rissuto, where an agitated throng of *contadini* swarmed at dawn in front of the administrator's offices, in an atmosphere reminiscent of the western American pioneers. Then we turned back northward, crossing the Rocca di Neto reserve and passing through Strongoli, among nameless hills that succeed each other like petrified waves in a perilous sea, till we came to the lonely Torre Melissa; and we climbed up to Melissa itself, in a deserted and silent land of sticky clay. We made a lengthy stop at Melissa and discussed the situation with *contadini* and officials, in a strained atmosphere. Then we continued our journey along the coast as far as Corigliano, and came back to Cosenza through the Alba-

† If you had come with the reform law in your hand, we know where the credit for it lies: with the dead and wounded of Melissa, with the fight we have made and are still making.

nian villages, in the first shower of sleet, by night. Everywhere we had found peasants and officials confronting each other: peasants taking up different attitudes, and in varying conditions, but all of them— though in different ways—mistrustful toward this new situation, a situation they had been desiring for centuries, for which they had struggled, but in which, now that it had fallen from heaven like an unexpected paternal largesse, they were totally incapable of believing; officials who ought to have been working for them and with them, but who kept concealed within themselves an ancient hereditary hatred for the peasants, and who were led to make use of the new reform laws—they who belonged to the *petite bourgeoisie* of the villages—as a method of regaining their centuries-old, tottering prestige: these were ever-present, eyes wide open and ears pricked, with their carefully creased trousers, and their thin mustaches, all ready to reassert their own kind of control over the deserted and divided land. There was a feeling of suspense in the air, of confused uncertainty; and it seemed to me there could be no better way of describing this than by a remark from the letter of a friend of mine, which I quoted at the end of my article: "Do you happen ever to have seen, carried along on a stretcher, a person whose life or death are of interest not only to his family but to the whole village? A small southern village, I mean, where the women start screaming but do not move a finger, where the men crowd round, their hands dangling at their sides, where policemen and *carabinieri* rush to form a cordon and someone

13

has to go and look for the doctors at their homes and they arrive one by one and the disease and the presence of the poor man who is to be operated upon are discussed over and over again and he himself lies there, fierce-eyed, and does not speak or move, but, say the women, an angel and a devil are fighting over him?"

And so we went back to Cosenza, and at night I left again to catch the Rome train at Paola; I gave a lift to an old Lucanian peasant I knew, who expounded to me what the land reform really was and what it might have been, how it ought to have been the handiwork of the peasants, the fruit of the peasant movement, the main factor and moving force in their new relationship with the state. As I left this varying world of struggle and hope and disappointment, this domain of poverty and clay, this reservoir of human worth and courage, I took his words with me, words that had but one single meaning and one single name, and that was: self-government, peasant autonomy.

And so my story came to an end, with this affirmation of the value of peasant autonomy. For a long time I was uncertain as to whether to publish it here; and there were several reasons for doing so. In the first place it actually dealt with the same journey (as in reality it was) which had begun round about Etna and ended in a very different kind of country which was nevertheless close to Sicily and closely connected with it, and in which I was traveling with Sicily fresh in my memory. It seemed to me moreover that, even though the peasant problem in the Calabrian countryside has characteristics of its own which are different from the Sicilian problem, an analysis of it might possibly be of use to the reader, and might also give him a better understanding of the concluding section of the book, the account of the death of Salvatore Carnevale. But, on consideration, I felt that this piece was too different from the others, not merely because of the different country it describes, the different people and their different story, but, particularly, because of the difference in the occasion that had prompted me to write it as a precise, detailed report on the state of affairs in the first districts to be affected by land reform in the year 1952: and its literary style is therefore, naturally, different—in part, at least—from that of the other sections; its tone is that of an inquiry; in it the reader's attention is directed toward a problem—albeit toward the psychological and human reflections of that problem—rather than toward such signs of current events and affairs as the eye of the writer can discern, without prejudice or program, in the face of the countryside and of its people. Many of the ideas and observations which were then new and expressed for the first time have since come, during these last years, into current public use. In the end, therefore, I decided not to include it. Nevertheless, now that the book is made up and it is too late to change anything, I regret my decision, for a personal reason which bears in itself the sole responsibility—odd and inopportune though it may appear to my readers—for my making mention here of an article which does not form part of my book. This reason is my memory of Rocco Scotellaro, who was my companion on my journey through the country districts of Calabria. In my article I did not mention him; yet he was present in every page, in every word. He did not leave me for one moment during the brief progress through the districts affected by the land reform; and he insisted on taking notes for me, in his affectionate, modest, boyish way, writing them down, as his habit was, on little bits of paper, cigarette packets, matchboxes; he talked to the *contadini* with his own characteristic capacity for achieving a direct contact which succeeded without difficulty in opening even the tightest-closed mouths and minds, he debated with the abstract propagandists whom we found at Melissa, he sang with the Albanian singers when we stopped in the evening, with the first sleet falling cold on the plateau. It was he who, by making a direct assault upon him with compact arguments and an indignant denunciation of his abuse of authority, compelled the Sila Company's official at Melissa to admit his injustices in front of the assembled *contadini*. Perhaps I should have done well to rewrite and republish the whole fragment, including an account of him: of his arrival at Cosenza to meet me at the Albergo Imperiale after traveling all night from Naples; of the night we spent in the little hotel at Crotone after walking about the streets in the dark, beneath the walls of Baron Galluccio's great palace; of his youthful, expansive, poetical personality and his gift for friendly contact. It was his letter that I have already quoted, with its comparison of the land reform to the sudden illness of a peasant; and the ideas I expounded in my article on the subject of peasant autonomy were his also. I think this was the last journey we made together through the country districts near his own home, and it gives me pleasure to pause for a moment and recall it. I could describe many episodes during that journey with him, but shall limit myself to one.

When, after stopping for a short time at the office of the company's technicians and the so-called cooperative in Santa Severina, we were on the point of starting off again, in a tearing storm and a downpour of rain, toward Crotone, a young man came running up to tell me that the archbishop had heard of my visit and wanted to see me. In the piazza, between the castle and the archbishop's palace, the long threads of rain looked like a tissue of white strings in the light of the headlamps against the black background of the night. The archbishop's palace is an ancient building, architecturally fine but bleak and bare inside. Rocco, owing perhaps to some sort of youthful reserve, would not go up with me to see the archbishop but stayed waiting in the car. At the top of the stairs a young priest was awaiting me; he was almost a boy, with a smooth, rosy face and fair hair, and as he showed me, with greatest politeness and courtesy, into a large room, he told me that he, like me, came from Piedmont and that he had only been a short time with his excellency in this unknown country, also that he had already read my book on the South several times during the few months he had been here; it was almost his breviary. While he was talking in this way, the archbishop appeared in the doorway. At a glance he did not look more than thirty—tall, slim, extremely elegant in his black habit and red waistband, with graceful, polished movements and a fine, intelligent, strong-willed face, like a Stendhal hero who has dropped by chance into a desert. He treated me with exquisite politeness and told me that he too was Piedmontese, from my own neighborhood, and that, in this place, he felt as I must have felt at the time of my banishment, among these people who were so different and so mistrustful. He had read and reread my book, and kept it on the table beside his bed. The peasants here, he said, were good people certainly, but so suspicious. It was so difficult to get into contact with them, to penetrate their reserve. "If only," he added, smiling and rueful, "if only they were Piedmontese or Venetian peasants!" "If they were Piedmontese or Venetian peasants, excellency, the southern question would not exist," I answered in the same tone. With all the distress of a shepherd struggling to collect a scattered flock, he went on to tell me of the difficulty of overcoming the peasants' hostility; saying also that it was difficult to tell what even the Sila Company wanted; that one might be able to collaborate with them, but they were in the midst of a crisis now and were changing their directors; but the greatest difficulty lay in the feelings of the working people. "It is not for me to say this," I answered, "and I ask your pardon for doing so, excellency, but I should like to remind you that however

18

great a fund of love and Christian charity, of brotherly solidarity and help and goodness, is made available to the peasant population here, it will never be enough: to so many tyrannies and injustices have they been subjected, for centuries and centuries, by all the civil, military and—forgive my saying it—the ecclesiastical authorities as well. Because of this, believe me, excellency, whatever is done, it will never be enough." The archbishop shook his head in sign of agreement with these words of mine: "It is true, doctor, it is true," he said. It was time now for me to take my leave: I told him that a very dear friend of mine was waiting for me below, Rocco Scotellaro, the peasant writer and poet from Lucania, and I told him briefly about him. Since Rocco had not come up, the archbishop was kind enough to accompany me downstairs to the main door, so as to meet and greet him.

On other journeys through the land reform districts which I made later, Rocco was no longer with me. He was no longer with me, but in the cemetery at Tricarico beside the Basento River, when I went, the following year, to visit the village of La Martella, near Matera, of which we had so often spoken together. I almost felt that he was at my side when I went into the houses that had been built according to the abstract "peasants' house" plan devised by the architects. At one house I visited, the *contadino* was anxious to show me the stable. How often had Rocco told me of the peasant meetings at Matera, with their discussions about cows and mules—interminable, serious discussions on genuine problems! The stable here was splendidly clean and tidy, and in the middle of it stood a big white cow, bright and shining with a chaplet of flowers on her head between her long, pale horns, chewing her cud in a leisurely, haughty fashion, like a queen. She was a wonderful cow, but the *contadino* explained to me that he found her very expensive, not merely because she had been debited against him at the price of one hundred and eighty thousand lire by the land reform office, which had assigned her to him compulsorily—as they had done also to the other *contadini* of the village—but because he had to keep her, to buy fodder in order to feed her, and could make no use of her. "If only she was a milch cow, but she's just a working cow, and the land they've assigned to me is four hours away from here, and I can't make the cow walk all the way there and then work. So we keep her in the stable. She's a beautiful cow, there's no denying it, and she serves as an ornament. We wanted to have some mules, or else milch cows, but they sent these from Rome without asking our opinion, and we've got to keep them, and feed them, and we can't even resell them, because that's forbidden." I asked him what he called this wonderful cow of his. "Bellavita," he answered. "I call her Bellavita because she's the only person *che faccia la bella vita*—who lives well—in this village."

Rocco Scotellaro was no longer with me then. I should like not merely to recall him and greet him here, but to talk about him at greater length, about the poet of peasant freedom. But his book *L'Uva puttanella* is being published shortly, at the same time as this book of mine—two years after his death —and in the preface I have written for it I have spoken of his true worth and of what he was to the peasant world. These lines hold no more than a memory of him and a regret.

Now that I have allowed myself (and I hope the reader will forgive me) to make a few observations upon a piece of writing that he will not read, I feel encouraged to add yet one more episode of that same journey in Calabria. During the evening at Cosenza, when Rocco had not yet arrived from Naples, I was wandering about the town by myself and came by chance into the neighborhood of the railway, into a half-dark street bounded on one side by the railway embankment, from which it was separated by a wooden fence. Standing against this fence were several peddlers, who were crying up their wares underneath the acetylene lamps. Groups of peasants were listening to them attentively and silently, in astonished wonder at the trifles which were being offered with such real eloquence. A fustian-clad man behind a little table was displaying some pocketbooks. They cost, not a thousand lire, or five hundred, or two hundred or even one hundred and fifty; they cost only one hundred lire. "Look," he was saying, "they're made of artificial leather, and they've got everything you want; they've got two pockets. In this one you can put your small change, and your documents and tickets and identity cards; and in the

21

other you can put your banknotes, your ten and five thousand lire notes—or if you haven't got any, your thousand lire notes; and if you haven't got any of them, then you can put your landlord's letters into it, your expulsion orders, your I.O.U.s, the accounts of what you owe the Sila Company; and if you haven't got them either, then you can put your despair into it, and mine too. Look, they're only one hundred lire: and all lined with silk."

But why should I stop and describe things which are not even connected with Sicily, when I am well aware of the infinite number of things that happened to me in the island itself or that are concerned with it, and which I have not mentioned—so much so that I might begin the book all over again and rewrite it quite differently, write another book, in fact?

One day in 1948, long before the years about which I have written here, I was in my study in the Palazzo Altieri, now destroyed, busily occupied in writing *The Watch*, when there came to see me a Sicilian lawyer. He told me, in a slightly mysterious way, that he was the bearer of a message. Certain friends of his, whose names he could not give, and who, for no fault of their own, now found themselves a long way from their native villages, in the mountains of the interior, had heard that I had written a book in which the South was mentioned, and *contadini*, and brigands; and they thought they would like to give a big shooting party in my honor, and they were inviting me through him, he being

22

their lawyer. They were inviting me as friends, and I could go in perfect safety.

"Underneath here it doesn't rain," was the message brought to me by the lawyer; and as he said it he raised his right hand horizontally, at the same time touching its palm with the forefinger of his left hand. This signified friendship, and protection: beneath the shelter of their hand no rain could reach me.

I accepted the invitation joyfully. They were, the lawyer told me, a small band of brigand-peasants, forced to take to the mountains to defend themselves from the bands of real brigands. Their chief was a peasant, a natural poet who expressed himself in spontaneous verse. One day he had gone into the inn in his own village and there had found a drunken stranger who was demanding more drink and violently threatening the landlady. He had seized him by the jacket and thrown him out of the door, but, as he did this, he had suddenly understood, and had said to himself: "I am dead." Too late, he had recognized the drunken man: he was the most terrible, the most ferocious bandit of those years just after the war—a real traditional bandit who used to cut in pieces prisoners seized, held for ransom, and commit all sorts of outrageous acts of cruelty.

The peasant hurried home to fetch his gun and then fled into the open country. During the night, from behind a haystack, he saw the band who were searching for him to kill him as they rode by on horseback. "They were riding on stars," he recounted later, for he had seen, from his hiding place, the sparks beneath the shoes of the galloping horses. And so, to escape from the bandits, he had turned bandit himself; and he was soon joined by friends and relations, and by other landless peasants, and a new band was born.

The bandit whom he had insulted was later killed by his own lieutenant in a nocturnal tommy gun duel in a wood, after a quarrel over a woman and over the division of booty. The lieutenant took his place, but was soon ambushed and arrested while asleep, and was handcuffed and taken to the police station before being transferred to Palermo. He asked to go out on the balcony, and his request was granted. The street was full of people, both peasants and gentry. He looked at them all with contempt, and said: "I spit in their faces, the whole lot of them"; and then allowed himself to be led off to prison.

Although his enemies had disappeared, the brig-and-peasant was still unable to return home: he and his band were wanted men now, even though—according to what the lawyer told me—they had caused no bloodshed.

I accepted his invitation with enthusiasm. They would telegraph me a date on which I was to betake me to the lawyer's house, and the latter would then conduct me to join them for the shooting party. The telegram, sent off on December 2nd, gave me an appointment for the 7th; but it was not delivered to me until the 9th. I could not therefore go, and sent my apologies. I heard later that they had at first been offended by my absence, but had afterward accepted—though with some difficulty—my excuses. The shooting party had taken place just the same; they had killed one hundred and fifty quails and I don't know how many pheasants and other birds. For me they had provided a deserted house, with a wonderful bed; they had commandeered linen sheets and feather mattresses. Since I was not there, they had made the lawyer read my book to them in the evenings round the fire, when they came back from shooting; and the party had gone on for seven days, as long as was necessary to finish the reading of the book. They promised me another shooting party, as soon as it could be managed. But it never could be managed: they were induced, by a false promise that they would go unpunished, to come down from the mountains, and were thrown into prison.

I could go on for hours telling countless other true stories of this kind, stories so true that they seem unbelievable. But let us return to those other stories, equally true but more easily credible because they are written and documented with hardship and hunger and courage (and sometimes with blood and death). Let us return to our notes.

Since I finished writing the story of Salvatore Carnevale and his death, and of his mother and her denunciation, and of the Sciara feudal estate, today, the 21st of September, 1955, I read in the papers that a member of the Mafia belonging to Cerda has been found dead in a well, his hands tied behind his back, and that it is presumed that he was the actual perpetrator, or one of the actual perpetrators, of

Carnevale's murder; and it is supposed that he was eliminated by order of the Mafia itself, which thus seeks, by suppressing its own instrument, to obliterate all proofs and to avoid the lawsuit which is in preparation at Palermo. In the meantime the killing of peasants who were union organizers continues, the same bold and mysterious method being always used. The latest, so far, of these murders happened quite recently at Cattolica Eraclea, a village of the same type as Sciara, not far from Agrigento.

Sicily, like the whole of the South—but in its own particular way—is on the move; and the acts, the words, the feelings, the struggles, the expectations, the deaths of which I have spoken here, and all the other, countless things that occur every day in the towns of the coast and the villages of the interior, are moments in its development. Profound problems present themselves and seek solution, every day, through the life and the blood of human beings. Here, in this little book, they are but lightly touched upon, taken for granted as framework of my story. I hope to be able to give a more complete picture of them later on, in another book or in possible future editions of this one. My kind readers must therefore be content, for the present, with the little that I am offering them here, which is but a first, rapid picture of a world that is changing from one day to another and becoming bravely conscious of its own existence.

Rome, September 1955

ONE

1

As soon as the car bringing the mayor of New York—
a fine gray Pontiac borrowed for the occasion—had
stopped at the entrance to the village of Isnello, and
Signor Impellitteri and his signora had got out, amid
the clamor of applause and the clash of the town
band, into a confused mass of policemen, motorcyclists, journalists, photographers, inquisitive spec-
tators, infinite cousins and second cousins and other
relations, townsmen, peasants, shepherds, women,
and, in fact, the whole 4,000 inhabitants of Isnello
who were all waiting for him, the village boys
crowded round it, yelling to each other, pushing and
knocking against each other, elbowing a way through
so as to touch it. *"Toccamo 'a macchina!*—let's touch
the car!" they shouted, egging one another on, with
the serious expressions of people who are doing
something important. "Let's touch the car, *and then
we shall get to America!"* The car had only just
arrived, and already it had become a relic, a thing

holy and miraculous, which if merely touched would have the power to ensure that these children, intent, now, on their extempore ritual, would attain the truest paradise of all, the longed-for paradise of America. The car remained there, stationary, all day long. Thousands of childish hands reverently touched it, thousands of wide black eyes gazed at it with passion and hope. On the first house in the village, immediately above the car, was an inscription in large letters which time had failed to expunge, one of those maxims signed with a huge M with which Mussolini covered all the walls of Italy: *Peoples whose cradles are empty have no right to Empire.* The cradles of Isnello are not empty—far from it: the streets swarm with children: but empire does not now mean (and has never meant) anything but a desire to escape, a desire that places trust in a magical hope, in a childish propitiatory rite.

And so, from the very first moment of his entry, Signor Impellitteri's visit was, for the peasants of Isnello, a fabulous adventure, a mythological occurrence. I do not know whether Signor Impellitteri was conscious of this. On the whole I think not: he is too physically close to that world to be able to perceive its nature. I do not know, and I did not ask him, the reasons that sent him on his journey to Italy (and to Palestine): whether it was a straightforward taste for seeing other countries, or a desire to tighten the bonds of friendship between Italy and America, or a quest for popularity and a wish to do something that would please his electors, or an affectionate curiosity to become acquainted with his own native place, to show it to his wife and to pay homage to the memory of his parents, or all these things combined. If he had been born in a large town, or in a small town or modern village in northern Italy, his journey would be no more than an item of the ordinary political news which figures transiently in the newspapers for a day, or would be merely a matter of his own private and special sentimental interest, with which it would be both useless and indiscreet of us to concern ourselves. Instead of which, this journey has become, for the people of Isnello, a myth; and so it will remain, for all time, though this had been neither intended nor foreseen: the myth of birth and of fortune, the myth of America, of the other face of the world. There is no doubt that Signor Impellitteri (whether through cleverness or simplicity, I do not know) did all that was required to bring the myth into being; from this point of view he behaved quite perfectly. Furthermore not only he, but everybody, behaved quite perfectly: the peasants, the gentry, the authorities, the Christian Democrat delegates of both sexes, the Communists, the priests, the relations, and even the goats and the donkeys, and the dogs, and even the flies. For it was at Isnello that the whole tale was unfolded, in one of the many thousands of villages of that ancient, simple-hearted land, where all things become true, even the journeys of politicians.

The affair began, to tell the truth, in the most conventional manner. American and Italian journalists, photographers and the various authorities had already made an assault, several days beforehand, on all the possible means of transport from Rome to Palermo. Airplanes, sleeping cars and even the old steamer that does the nightly service between Naples and the Conca d'Oro, had all been fully booked up for several days, for not only was the mayor of New York going to Sicily, but at the same time there were also going there the candidates in a beauty competition the winner of which was to be proclaimed "Miss Europe." Failing the regular plane, I found myself leaving on an extra plane, in which it so happened that Signor Impellitteri himself was traveling, together with his charming wife with the periwinkle-blue eyes, and also some of the so-called European beauties. I shall not stop to describe Signor Impellitteri, because everyone knows him. As for the girls, they were, as someone unkindly remarked, not all of them, strictly speaking, girls; and they had been picked up all over the place, to represent the most unlikely states—Bulgaria, the principality of Monaco, Liechtenstein. There they sat, all to one side, with their unreal, rather frightened faces. When we arrived at Palermo there were more photographers, more officials, more journalists, and the first troop of the mayor's cousins: a great quantity of Impellitteris, of Fiorentinos, of Vaccas and Cannicis, who had come from all parts of Sicily to greet their illustrious relation. From the airfield we were all taken to a large hotel dating from the beginning of this century, a mixture of Moorish and *art nouveau,* where more photographers, more journalists, more officials, more Impellitteris were waiting. The mayor was immediately dragged off into the whirl of a full day of official receptions; I myself was beset by some of the shyer members of the Impellitteri clan who had taken me for an intimate friend of their grand relation and who, displaying their identity cards and documents to me, begged me to introduce them to him. One of them, who had two little twin boys as crosseyed as the paladin Roland, detained me and said he would like to show me the "gynacological" tree of the family. It was with some difficulty that I managed to get away from him, deferring my studies of the Impellitteri genealogy till later; I then got into my car and fled away in the direction of Isnello.

The first part of the road, as far as Termini Imerese, passes along the most splendid coastline in all Italy. A marvelous sea shines through orange groves and tall reeds; men and women are working in the sunshine in the vegetable gardens; at small, hand-operated kilns workmen are pounding up earth for the making of tiles; endless numbers of painted carts, gaily decorated with the stories of the paladins, pass along the roads like a continuous emigration of a people that cannot keep still. But, a few miles beyond Termini Imerese, the road turns inland toward the mountains. The landscape changes all at once, and one comes into the immense, bare moorlands of the feudal estates. These are the lands of princes and barons, of the Principe di Gangi, of the Marchese di Santa Colomba. As one rises, gradually, by the road that makes the circuit of the Madonia Mountains—the road upon which the noblemen of Sicily like killing themselves in motor races—nature assumes the solemn, grand, desolate appearance of the Italian interior, of the Italy of the peasants. At Collesano a crowd of boys was awaiting us in the piazza, and Armando, the village idiot, a man already well advanced in years, welcomed us with a cheer and prostrated himself on the ground in front of us, under the fatherly eye of the superintendent of police. Beyond Collesano one enters a mountain gorge, between the high walls of the Madonia Mountains, and the road continues to rise until, at a bend, the village of Isnello becomes visible in the distance. A flock of sheep was blocking the road, together with shepherds and dogs. An old woman went past carrying a bundle of sticks. On the black veil that covered her head, on her back, on her skirt, an innumerable company of flies clung to her and were carried along, motionless and quiet. As I looked from there at the village, there came back to me the familiar picture of a small village in Lucania. Isnello resembled it, even though larger, less poor, cleaner. It is a village of shepherds, of peasants who are landowners on the smallest possible scale, the ground being divided up into microscopic sections, of craftsmen whose crafts are now fallen into decay, but who remember the golden age when splendid lace was made here, when bells were cast and skins were dressed and glass was blown. Even today the three parts into which the village is divided are called *Vetreria, Fonderia* and *Conceria.*

The history of this village (as of all the others) has hitherto been merely prehistoric. The passage of time has brought with it no events but the change of its feudal lords—Saracens, Aragonese, Bourbons, the princes of Santa Colomba and the counts of Isnello: but (again like the others) it is of great antiquity and therefore full of a profound nobility. And the humanist priests of the last century who lived there, Don Carmelo Virga or Don Cristoforo Grisanti, wrote learned volumes on the history of this village without a history, debating upon its Pelasgic or Sicanian origins and upon the Syriac or Oriental etymology of its name, upon the passing of some prince or other and upon its changeless customs. Will some other priest add to these volumes a last learned chapter on the events of tomorrow?

The village had already been invaded by American journalists, who were going from door to door questioning the inhabitants with a sort of mania for even the most futile items of news. They wanted to know everybody's Christian names and surnames, their ages and their jobs and their earnings, the number of people in the family and, of course, their degree of relationship to Signor Impellitteri. It was like a large-scale detective inquiry, to which these *contadini* submitted with resigned and well-bred courtesy. The reporters' notebooks became crammed with useless information, while the town crier blew his trumpet and shouted his proclamation at every street corner: "Tomorrow the mayor of New York is arriving; all animals—donkeys, goats, sheep and pigs—are to be shut

35

up in the houses and are not to walk on the public road." The town clerk and the beadle were going round with a bundle of old, faded flags with which to adorn windows and balconies—the eighty little flags used at the feast of St. Nicholas of Bari, the patron saint of Isnello. The female cousins of the mayor were decorating the doors of their houses with simple festoons of leaves. In the road, near the entrance to the village, laborers were hurriedly filling in the holes in the surface, and a young man was polishing one of the many little figures of the Madonna that stand here and there in wayside shrines. The municipal road sweeper and his four improvised assistants were applying themselves, with their brooms, to a task which was unending, since the animals were not yet shut up; and they would have to start all over again at dawn next day. The town band was rehearsing in front of the church. But everything was calm, there was no sign of excitement: it was an ordinary working day, and, as always on working days, the village was half empty. The modest preparations were being carried out quietly, almost with indifference. Down the street were passing men who bore an extraordinary resemblance to Signor Impellitteri, having the same long, dark faces, the same black eyes, the same straight noses, and who nevertheless *were not his relations*. There was one, on the other hand, a tall man dressed in black—he, too, crosseyed like the paladin Roland—who came up to me and showed me his identity card: he was a cousin, and he had come from a village a very long way away, at the other end of Sicily.

The "Americans"—that is, inhabitants of Isnello who had lived in America and then come back to their native land—were walking about the piazza in their caps and their best suits and their gold watch-chains, waiting for the greatest of all "Americans," an American who, however, would not be remaining there. One of them, a sergeant who had served for many years as a regular in the American army, talked to me at great length about the needs of the village, about the landslip which had eaten up the forty million lire that should have been used for building the school, about the bad use of the money, and the hope that millions of dollars would come pouring down from heaven owing to the mayor's visit. But all this did not appear to move the peasants and shepherds of Isnello very deeply. The preparations that were being made differed in no way from those that are made for an ordinary *festa* for a saint or for the visit of a bishop or a prefect. But there was something else that moved them, something that was less evident and that they did not talk about, because they are as reserved as they are courteous. There was something mysterious about this man Impellitteri whom they were awaiting, and whom no one knew, because he had been taken away as a baby of one year old, fifty years ago; and who was now returning, surrounded with glory like a saint from paradise, from America: and who, though unknown to everybody,

37

was nevertheless one of them. There was something mysterious about his birth, as about that of Homer, and of Christopher Columbus (or, to be more precise, of Jesus Christ); and there was something miraculous about his return and his approaching epiphany.

As with those great men of antiquity, or, better still, with Jesus Christ, so does a dense cloud of legend cover his birthplace. He was born, so the records say, in a street which was then called Via Figurella and which is now called Via Cristoforo Grisanti, *Folkrorista* (the eminent "folklorist" is thus commemorated at the corner of the street, with a pardonable spelling mistake), right at the corner of a very narrow lane which—not without profound and obvious reason—is called Bethlehem Lane: but it is not known whether he was born at No. 70 or No. 67 in this street. I was welcomed at the door of No. 67 by the wife of the road sweeper, a small, very dark woman, still young, with shining eyes and features of great refinement, a woman who seemed to be quivering with hidden passion, with a secret fanaticism: she was surrounded by a large number of children. "They try to make out," she said to me, "that he was born over there, at the house opposite, at No. 70; but it's *here* he was born. This was his only home, and that's absolutely sure, sure as the Blessed Sacrament. Here he was born, in this house, in a room full of straw and hay, like the Child Jesus. I don't know anything about it, I was born only yesterday, but *that's what the old ones say*. His birth took place here: I don't know anything, it doesn't interest me, I'm no one of importance. It's an honor, of course, it's a great honor; but I was born only yesterday, I'm just a tenant here, and I don't know anything. But that's what the old ones say, that he was born here, here at No. 67. People claim now that he was born at No. 70, and there have been quarrels, because people believe that he will leave a lot of money. There's envy. I don't ask for anything, my husband's work gives me enough to eat, he's the road sweeper. But you see, they might at least pave the street in front of No. 67; they didn't do it because of the great envy there was. It's like the political parties, you know what the parties are like; they're all the same. You're a Democrat, you're a Communist, you're a Socialist, you're something else—that's how the lies get started. When he arrives tomorrow, I don't want him to come either here or there, not to either place: but I don't know anything about it, I was born only yesterday. It's an honor, of course, it's a very great honor; but that's all there is to it."

In front of No. 70 there was a woman with a beard who sought to conceal her face in a black shawl. And there were two old women of ninety, and other women, and peasants and children. Their historical documentation was better. One old woman, with pale blue eyes and a big wart at the root of her nose, asserted that she had a perfectly clear memory of Impellitteri's father, who kept, she said, his shoemaker's bench on that very doorstep, and when it was fine he put it outside, and when it rained he put it inside. And she remembered when he went to America, "looking for a piece of bread." Her own son was also in America, at "Schenicchi" (Schenectady): and she showed me photographs of her son with his wife and his American family. Another old woman, daughter of one of the witnesses of the birth, assured me that she remembered that he had been born here, at No. 70. And she went into the house in search of a proof, of an indisputable document. And there, framed in a wooden frame, was a certificate of membership of the Eucharistic League, dated 1897, on behalf of Nicolina Di Maria, formerly Vincenzo, the mayor's grandmother; and it had been left to her—as a souvenir by the Impellitteris on the day they started for America. I asked the old woman what she had given in exchange to these venerable emigrants. She hesitated a little before answering, as though she were ashamed, and then said: "I gave them some cheese to eat on the voyage; they were poor, they hadn't any money."

An American journalist with a mustache, who came up at this moment, interrupted us in order to note down everyone's name in his notebook—like an examining magistrate—and inquired: "What do you hope the mayor of New York will do tomorrow?" "What can he do?" they replied. "We can't say, we don't know anything about it." "So many things are needed," said an old man, "a hospital, because now we have to go to Palermo or Cefalù; there was an old legacy, but it disappeared; and a school, and a town hall, and a religious cinema—" (there is no

40

cinema at Isnello, and the old man would like there to be a religious one). They answered him just in order to please him, but one could see that they were proud and full of dignity, and that in reality they were not hoping for anything; they were neither asking nor expecting anything, neither presents nor charities, nothing practical, in any case, nothing belonging to this earth. They were expecting simply that he would come, they were expecting a vision. But a little boy cried out: "The band, the band!" His dream was that Impellitteri would give money for a fine brass band; for saints are known to love music.

Not only the place but also the day of the mayor's birth is wrapped in mystery. For it appears that Impellitteri has always kept the 4th of February as his birthday; but in the precious papers that the town clerk showed me he is registered as having been born on the 4th of January, 1900, at 7:15 in the morning —the first-born of the century in the commune of Isnello. With him the century opens; but was he really born in this century, or in some remote period of antiquity? Of his birth, and of his return, the old ones, as the road sweeper's wife said, had made a fable.

Enveloped in this mythological mist and in the darkness which had now fallen, I hastened away in the car down the long road toward Palermo, among the dangling lanterns of the carts and the doleful singing of their drivers. In the garden of the Moor-

41

ish hotel, by the light of arc lamps, those seven poor girls were filing past half-naked, like pink frogs, in front of the mayor of New York, and under the starved and greedy eyes of the nobility of Palermo.

2

The sun rose, next morning, with all the brilliance
and cheerfulness suitable to a holiday; but it was already high in the heavens when I awoke, for the
porter at this grand hotel had forgotten, with truly
Saracen indifference, to call me; and Signor Impellitteri and his *cortège* had already departed. I set out
in pursuit, leaving behind me in a flash Ficarazzi
and Ficarazzelli and Bagheria and Trabia and
Termini Imerese, flying along among the painted
carts as if I had been taking part in some absurd
American film. I caught him up at last, at a level
crossing where the road begins to climb, because the
procession, which was accompanied by three motorcyclists from the municipality of Palermo wearing
enormous black and white helmets, was advancing
slowly in order to give the illustrious visitors leisure
to enjoy the scenery; and we went on together up
the bends of the mountain road.

If Isnello, the day before, had looked like all

peasant villages, half-deserted, today, on the other hand, its little streets were not wide enough to contain the crowd. They were all there, peasants and shepherds and artisans and women, behind the town band and the town flag, squeezed together and lined up into a wall of faces, as in a religious pageant. Isnello is noted for its ancient popular pageant of the drama of the Passion, performed in a large number of tableaux and called the *Casazza,* which has been held, for some centuries, during Holy Week, in years of good harvests, when there is more money. All the peasants take part in it as actors, and there are to be seen Jesus and Saint Joseph and Mary and Herod and Pilate and the Roman soldiers and the Jews and the apostles. The scene today was the most extraordinary of all *Casazzas.* Today, too, they were all actors, but there was a real protagonist: after the flight into Egypt fifty years ago, it was the entry of Christ into Jerusalem.

Beneath the broad strips of cloth upon which was written, in the dubious English of the "Americans," "WELCOME IMPY," "WELCOME IN YOUR NICE COUNTRY," beneath the loaded balconies and the darting glances of the girls looking down from them, amid music and applause, the mayor and his escort proceeded up the whole length of the Corso in order to go and hear Mass at the Mother Church. At the end of the Corso, at the turning toward the church, there were hundreds of women drawn up in rows, with black veils on their heads, a wall of faces and of bright black eyes, just under-

44

neath the side of a house upon which was written up "MEAT," and with the wasted, bare slope of the mountainside close behind. From the silent group rose a voice, lonely and piercingly shrill: "Vincenzino! Joy of your mother's heart! Here stand the women of Isnello! Look at us, Vincenzino!" It was a woman wearing the same black veil as the peasant women and standing with arms outstretched. I looked at her and recognized her as a competent woman deputy, a valiant member of our government. Signor Impellitteri turned; and his eye rested benevolently upon the applauding women.

It was difficult to get into the church owing to the great crowd. There were no four-legged creatures in the street, neither donkeys nor goats nor sheep, all of whom had been banned by proclamation: on the other hand there were flies, the lazy, patient flies of early autumn, glorious victors in so many battles, in innumerable swarms; and they went with us into the beautiful fifteenth century church, which was once a mosque (perhaps they also wished to pay homage to the mayor and to God), flying in thousands through the air that was filled with organ notes and settling resolutely upon the faces of the faithful, upon the kneeling officials, upon the American journalists, upon the cameras, upon the policemen, upon the helmeted motorcyclists, and even upon the fine, prophet-like face and great white beard of an illustrious friar, a native of Isnello, Father Domenico, general of the Capuchins, who had come specially from Rome. A bull-necked young priest with dark glasses and a green stole officiated; he too was a cousin of Signor Impellitteri. The Mass was long and solemn: the mayor, in the front row, crossed himself by bringing the thumb of his right hand to his mouth, according to the time-honored custom of the Isnello women at the approach of thunder, to avert a storm.

Beside me was a young man with a black mustache as thin as a thread, whom I had already encountered in the hotel at Palermo: evidently he was a policeman in Signor Impellitteri's escort, and—I do not know how—had recognized me. "Tell me," he now whispered to me, "you who are a writer, how does one set about publishing a novel? I want to write one; I've had six years of imprisonment, and I've seen a lot of things. But how does one set about getting it published? Whom does one approach? I don't know anything about it. But you must know . . ." So the policeman, too, felt himself to be an artist. While I was explaining to him, in a whisper, that publishing firms exist, we were interrupted by the long, lean cousin with the crosseyes whom I had seen the day before, the one who had come from a long way off. He had an extremely sad face. "With all these people," he said to me, "I dare not introduce myself. He hasn't even seen me. *You* must tell him I'm here! I am the only real Impellitteri, the others are all Billitteri. You must tell him!" But how was I to tell him? The Mass was coming to a close, and, after a speech of salutation from the priest ("Fifty years ago he came in here as a baby to be regenerated by the waters of baptism. Who would ever have

46

thought that fifty years later he would come back as mayor of the greatest city in the world? This is a miracle of faith. May this same faith shine forth for the benefit of the Church and the nations!"), everyone moved toward the door.

After the birth in God, the birth to the world; after the house of God, the house of the state: we had to go to the town hall, only a few yards away. We reached it with difficulty, for the crowd was even thicker: the whole street was a sea of happy faces. The town hall consists of two small rooms on the first floor of an old house, to which one climbs up a steep staircase. There we were shown the precious papers, the birth certificate, the request for an emigration visa made by the mother of little Vincenzino and signed by her—since she was illiterate—with a cross. There, too, souvenirs were presented to the visitor—a large photograph of Isnello framed in silver, a sentimental novel written by a woman of Isnello and entitled *Torna per loro!*, and, lastly, a silver casket full of Isnello earth, with an engraved inscription upon it: "A gift from the commune of Isnello to its great son Vincenzo Impellitteri." This handing over of earth was an ancient feudal custom. The priest Grisanti, in one of his learned books, in a chapter entitled "Awesome memories," says: "I was told as a young man, by persons of eighty or more years old, that when the lord and master (so they called the count of Isnello) returned to Isnello after a long absence, the magistrates of the commune, according to the law, had to go to the great gate of

47

the village (recently pulled down) in order to receive him and deliver a handful of earth to him in a cup, together with the keys of the gate, in sign of vassalage." Signor Impellitteri did not receive the keys, because they do not exist, but he received the earth, as was right, because he was entering his village as something more than a count or a feudal lord, as a mayor from America, a king of heaven.

Then, from the balcony overlooking the street the official speeches began: one by the representative of the province, one by the mayor of Isnello, and then Mr. Impy's reply. It would be all too easy to be ironical at the expense of this oratory: there would be no need for the pen of the Gogol of *Dead Souls:* all that would be required would be to transcribe here—if it existed—the shorthand version of the speeches, without any alteration. But I shall not do this, because it would not be fair. These speeches, in spite of their pompous rhetoric, were, in their way, perfect. The representative of the provincial council spoke of the pride of the poor emigrant, who had become illustrious "not through descent from noble loins, but through the two laws of Sicily—the law of honor and the law of love." And he spoke of how "the personal pride of Impellitteri is both soothed and enlarged in the pride of the four thousand citizens of Isnello, and, if you will allow me to say so, of the four millions of Sicilians. . . . You have shown," he went on, "what is the true meaning of our empire and of the rule of our people, the highest product of its civilization. You, a true Sicilian from your very cradle, a Sicilian by your birth certificate, are one of those wonderful colonists who, having plowed the waves which today you traversed again with the flight of an eagle, have established our empire: the empire of toil. I have to thank you, my dear Vincenzo, in the name of everyone, because everyone feels, in your person, the triumph of his own race. And this has come about because in New York there is freedom and equality . . ." And so on.

Apart from the empire and the cradle (the same ones that I had seen on the wall, with the signature M.), apart from the triumph of the race, the orator had said one true thing: the village of Isnello was celebrating in its own honor; each one of them, in Impellitteri, recognized himself. He was like Christ, a God-Man; and it was on account of his ordinary human nature—his Sicilian and Isnellese nature, in fact—that all of them, of all classes, honored and adored him: because he was a man like other men, a Sicilian like other Sicilians. The same things were said, in a simpler and less emphatic manner, by the mayor of Isnello, a schoolmaster: he felt himself a colleague of Signor Impellitteri, and therefore more familiar, on more equal terms, and more proudly and naturally happy.

I do not know whether Signor Impellitteri is a good speaker in English: in Sicilian he was perfect. He realized that his fellow citizens were celebrating themselves in him, and he established, in a few words, all the elements necessary to crystallize a myth in which the shoemaker's son might well take the place of the Carpenter's Son. He began by saying that he was happy to come back, as mayor of New York, to the town of his "nativity." It may have been a scanty knowledge of Italian, it may have been profound intuition; but he said, then and always, "nativity" instead of "birth," thus accepting, without realizing it, the realm of myth, and entering into it once and for all. He spoke about his wife and about his "papà and mamà," saying: "I am the son of a poor shoemaker who left Isnello without two pennies in his pocket, with five sons, and then a girl arrived: here, they were all boys, and in America a girl. It all goes to show that, with democracy, it is possible for these lads who are here now to become mayor of Rome tomorrow, or the head of the Italian state or the mayor of New York like me. That is democracy and freedom. I was baptized here, and now I am mayor of the greatest city in the world. Long live Sicily, long live Italy, long live the United States of America!"

Underneath the balcony, in the street, in the sunshine and the swarms of flies, everybody was happy, everybody was, in him, in the earthly paradise. His words had the same meaning as those which had been heard a thousand times: "The kingdom of heaven is open for all"; but the kingdom of heaven had come down onto that balcony, had become incarnate in one of themselves, and it was called America.

Honor having been paid to Church and state, it remained now, in order to complete the great homecoming, to proceed to the house of the nativity. It had been decided (some future apocryphal Gospel will be required to uphold the theory of No. 67) that this was the house at No. 70, at the corner of Bethlehem Lane; and in truth it was but a hut, even if the ox and the ass were not there, nor the straw in the manger, but merely the eternal, innumerable flies. A man from Calabria lives there, who earns three thousand lire a year by doing some sort of little job: only a few people could go in at a time because, they said, the floor was dangerous and would not stand the weight. Bare walls, a ceiling made of reeds, religious pictures pinned up here and there, a bed the only piece of furniture and, in place of a wardrobe, the rough branch of a tree upon which hang the humble garments of the family.

In front of this hut the wise men and the shepherds stood still, in adoration.

And here, with the adoration and the nativity, ended the sacred pageant in which Signor Impellitteri had found himself both protagonist and actor. No crucifixion, no Golgotha awaited him, however; merely a large luncheon, which was not the Last Supper but a luncheon organized by the nuns of the Santa Maria Orphanage; and after the luncheon, visits to relations; all of them things in which Signor Impellitteri went back to being just Signor Impellitteri. This was the conventional, private part of the visit: the sun, which up till now had been shining joyfully, retired, and soon the first autumn rain began to fall.

The orphan girls were waiting for him, before the

luncheon, singing a little song written specially for the occasion; and a little girl presented him with some flowers, saying as she did so:

> *Son troppo piccina*
> *Parlare non so*
> *Ma un piccolo dono*
> *Donare ti vo.* *

At this point Signor Impellitteri, a human being again, was unable to restrain his emotion and started shedding warm tears.

But luncheon was awaiting us. The journalists and the policemen were put into a small room apart; the Impellitteris of Palermo, who were not known to those of Isnello, and who had come in the last of the escorting cars, were left outside the door; and the cross-eyed twins and their father had to be content—since there is no hotel or inn at Isnello—with standing there and eating some bread and cheese. We, on the other hand, had an extremely good meal, and at the end of it there were sweetmeats made by the nuns, different kinds of nougat and *mocatoli* prepared by Sister Maria Benigna, Signor Impellitteri's cousin. Finally there were more speeches, including an extremely eloquent one by the lady under-secretary Signora Cingolani, who during the morning had been the one to cry out: "Vincenzino!" and who now had changed her peasant shawl for a more ministerial garb ("In that shawl," she said with a fine oratorical flour-

---

* I am too small, I cannot speak. But here is a little present which I wish to give you.

52

ish, "I felt I had spent the whole of my life"); she delivered a eulogy of Signora Impellitteri and ended by seeking to follow the Church tradition of transforming spontaneous myth into ecclesiastical ritual ("This day will remain in the memory of coming generations: you will be our protectors—our protector and protectress"), and of hanging up the holy pictures of St. Vincent and St. Elizabeth on the walls. At this point it was announced that Signor Impellitteri was giving half a million lire to his cousin's convent, and a million and a half to the commune, in order that, as the mayor of Isnello had advised, public shower baths should be constructed.

The gods, having become plain tutelary saints, had of course to perform their duty as protectors and philanthropists: but nevertheless I could not help wondering at the divine uselessness of the gift. Who will ever take a shower in Impy's shower baths? They will be, it is quite certain, an untouchable object of adoration.

It was raining hard now, with a cold autumnal rain, and the mountains were shrouding themselves in mist. Signor Impellitteri, a simple human being again, went and visited the houses of his relations, one by one, beginning with Sister Maria Benigna's convent. The American journalists were searching in vain for a telephone, for they were in an urgent hurry to telephone to New York without losing a minute; and they begged me to let them go off in my car: I myself would take their place in one of the cars of the escort. I started, in the rain, to wander all round the village, looking through doorways in lanes to where the goats were concealed; breathing in the smells, so familiar to me, of smoke and animals; going into the few shops. In the bar I came across the head of the Isnello Communists, a doctor, who was a member of the honorary reception committee and whom I had already seen at the luncheon at the orphanage. He too was pleased with the day. He told me that, in face of local events like that of today, which was an honor for everybody, all political differences came to a standstill. The only thing he had some doubts about was the shower baths, but this did not prevent his feeling that he too was a participant in the honor that was being conferred on everyone, that he too—just to the extent of one four-thousandth part—was mayor of New York.

Night had fallen, and we prepared to leave. As I was going toward the car, waiting for Signor Impellitteri to come out of the house of the last cousin, a *contadino* wearing an old military cape came up to me and said: "I want to get a job so as to get out of here. Any sort of a job. I'd willingly be a stoker on an engine, or a caretaker, or anything, so long as I can get away from this place."

We left, at last, in the dark. I found myself in the car belonging to the municipality of Palermo, together with the officials and other Sicilians of importance. As we crossed the dark expanses of the feudal estates, the conversation turned to the Mafia. The most important of my companions—he was the vice-mayor of Palermo, I think—said to me: "Do you really believe in those fairy stories? The Mafia does not exist, it's just a legend. There is no Mafia: if there were, it would be a very fine thing and I should be a member of it myself." We had now reached the coast. At Trabia the line of cars had to stop because a solemn procession was passing, amid flaring torches and exploding squibs. I got out to look. Long lines of men were walking in file amid volleys from the "Masculata": it was the procession of the Most Holy Crucifix. The archpriest, who was walking very slowly in front of the great Cross, was informed that Signor Impellitteri was in one of the stationary cars. He gave a start of pleasure and excitement, took off his hat out of respect, and, abandoning the Christ, began running toward the Pontiac. Here he paid his homage to Signor Impellitteri, and begged him to convey his personal greetings to Cardinal Spellman. "I have a cousin at Chicago too," he added. "Do you know him?" Signor Impellitteri did not know him.

Early the following morning I was plunged in the deepest sleep, in my room in the big Moorish hotel, when I was suddenly awakened by violent knockings on the door and the sound of someone coming in. I opened my eyes in the dim, early light and saw, beside my bed, a man of middling height and middle age, thickset, black of skin and black of eye, who said to me: "My name is Impellitteri!" He was a cousin, another cousin: I recognized him from his vaguely crooked eyes, like those of the paladin Roland. He wanted me to act as his go-between and introduce him to his cousin and speak to him about some pork

55

butcher's shop that he possessed: but sleep prevented me from listening to him. I dressed in haste, and fled. I wanted to go to Lercara Friddi (Lucky Luciano's native land), to see the sulphur mines. There I should encounter a truly different face of the world, a world of feudal monsters who dated back to a remote, unbelievable time and were yet still alive today and locked in a fierce struggle with the gaunt sulphur miners. A different world was opening, a different Sicily, although the two were contemporary. Impellitteri had gone.

3

A different hired car was awaiting us in the garden of the hotel. Its driver, too, was a different one from yesterday's, who had been a pompous old man, as affected and servile as a major-domo, accustomed to taking princes and Americans for motor trips and to giving stereotyped explanations, in an officious manner, about anything he was asked. Today's driver, on the other hand, was a young, fair man in a sweater, proud of his ramshackle old car and quite ready to open his heart to us with boyish charm. I had with me an interesting companion, Signor B., a very fine photographer, armed with magnificent instruments and gadgets, with miraculous filters and telephoto lenses: a Piedmontese with light hair and a pink face, calm and robust and used to wandering about the world and never being surprised at anything. He had heard of my plan of visiting a sulphur mine, and had asked if he might go with me. Since we thought we had plenty of time in front of us (Lercara is barely forty-five miles from Palermo), and he wanted to take some photographs, we decided to make a little tour, during the morning hours, in the neighborhood of Palermo before taking the road that leads toward Caltanisetta. Gianni, the driver, who was listening to us, broke in and suggested that we might go to Monte Pellegrino—for anyone who had never seen *that* had never seen anything. But we had already seen it: I had been, not long before, by the long road where the prickly pear gatherers pass with their baskets on their backs, right up as far as the statue of Santa Rosalia, the protectress, with its very long neck and strange goatlike face, standing out against the sky. I had seen, on the ground at its feet, two other heads, two gigantic heads of timeworn marble, covered with writing, with pencil scrawled or scratched signatures, two huge, abandoned heads. I had asked a man who, having finished his picnic lunch at the foot of the statue, was just going off down the hill again, what these fragments were. "Heads of Santa Rosalia which were struck off by lightning," he answered. "That's what they try to make out. Struck off by lightning, and each time she grew another head, did Santa Rosalia." And he added, with rationalistic prudence: "It can't really be so: it's a bit too much to believe. But that's what they try to make out." The little boy looked at him, as though scandalized by his skepticism, vague and restrained though it was, and I heard him say to his father who was holding him by the hand as they went off down the path, in a tone of reproof: "Papa, a miracle is a miracle!" And so we left

58

the mountain, and the miracles, and went down in the opposite direction, into the town.

We passed through a thickly populated quarter which they call "Stalingrado" and came out onto the waterfront, at Porta Carbone, which they call "the Kasbah." Here, among festoons of washing, we were surrounded by swarms of boys and small children: a little naked girl was trying to climb up onto a painted cart, old women with long, pale, haggard faces were sitting on doorsteps. A barber was shaving his customers in the street, under an awning supported on a stick. A gigantic woman was standing inside a hovel made of pieces of timber and petrol tins, with chairs and bits of broken furniture lying about, for some reason or other, on its roof: she was selling fruit, and made a movement of withdrawal when she felt herself being looked at. A round-eyed child, who looked like a frog, began jumping all about us, making faces, crouching down on the ground and leaping into the air so as to attract our attention. B. spoke of the slums and peripheries of the great cities he had visited; and Gianni, for whom this strange word seemed to have a different meaning, said: "This periphery is not a good one. If you want to see peripheries, there are plenty of them at Palermo. Even in the middle of the town. I know them all, the peripheries. If you like, I'll take you to some." We crossed the Via Roma and the Via Maqueda, we went past the crazy façade and the huge pillars, blown up like tires, of the main post office (behind which façade people are crowded together at a very small number of pigeonholes), and

59

very soon, after crossing other streets and lanes, reached the "periphery" of our driver's choice. Entrenched behind rags, beneath curtains and movable screens of sheets and shirts, women and children filled the alleyways. Vicolo Capraio, Vicolo del Forno ai Maestri d'Acqua, where the air has a secret look as it comes down green and gray into the narrow openings between the tall houses and little girls carry other, smaller girls in their arms: the spectacle is the same as in the *bassi* at Naples and in a hundred other places and towns in the South, and there is the same wretchedly poor but kindly crowd. In every doorway there is an artisan at work, surrounded by whirling throngs of children. In the windows appear women's faces, numerous enough to fill the whole window space, and bright, shining eyes, and wayward gestures. In a corner, in front of a pitch-dark little room, an old man was sitting on a broken-down chair, patiently making little figures of the paladins of France. He had a dish full of heads, as though for a cannibal feast, and he was threading them onto hooks at the neck, on the framework. There were other paladins, made of sugar, with wonderful colors and silver and gold armor and red and blue feathers on their helmets, in the little windows of various little shops, together with rosy naked women riding on cocks, and little figures of Bartali on his bicycle. These were the first to appear of the figures that are always given to children for All Saints' Day, the 1st of November; and people buy them by instalments, bringing five or ten lire when they can, until, by the end of October, they

finish paying—if they can—and take them home.
Here too we were accompanied by boys who pushed
and shoved each other, and here too there was one
who jumped about like a frog to attract attention to
himself. As we went along with this train of followers,
there suddenly appeared at a window, like a. vision,
the marvelously lovely face, pink and white and black,
and the shining hair and laughing eyes, of a girl
whose curiosity had been aroused. Followed by her
gaze, which triumphed over the surrounding poverty,
we rejoined the car which was awaiting us round the
corner of the lane.

B. suggested taking a run out along the coast road
—the same road that I had traversed twice the day
before—as far as Bagheria. He wanted to take advantage, for his work, of the sun which was now shining in the changeable sky among a trail of threatening clouds: and I agreed to this. We saw again, at the
edge of the road, the small kilns for handmade tiles
and bricks, and the half-naked workmen, intent upon
their craft among the tall flowering reeds with
plumes waving like fans in the sea breeze. The men
were covered with earth, their arms and hands were
encrusted with earth, there was earth on their tanned
faces, on their torn shirts, on their trousers, on their
bare feet; and they were nimble and quick and brilliantly skillful as they placed the earth on the convex
moulds, fined it down and smoothed it with light
touches of their hands, and cut it all around with a
wire, as the peasants of the Veneto cut *polenta*. Two
proprietor-craftsmen working together can make fif-

61

teen hundred tiles a day, between dawn and sunset. A worker on the other side of the road manages, alone, to produce five hundred a day, and receives two lire for each piece: but he works only when the weather is fine and the sun can dry the wet earth.

Farther on, groups of boys, men and women were busy making hempen ropes, round revolving cages in perpetual movement, pulling and twisting the yarn as they moved backward and intertwining the strands with their hands without ever pausing in their walk. Up and down, up and down, legs bare and bodies erect, eyes watchful and hands nimble—an antlike swarming of agile forms on the clear space of beaten earth. How many eyes, how many hands, how many countless individual tasks, with the simplest materials and the simplest, ancient tools; in the fields, also, and in the market gardens full of peasants stooping amid the dark green of orange and lemon groves and the rows of vegetables! In the sky, over the sea, urged on by the cool autumn wind, the first flocks of quails, coming from who knows where, and tired with their long journey from far-off lands, passed by in orderly ranks, in flight or battle formation; and the eye of the hunter followed them, from doorways of huts or from the road. A few belated boats, painted with sirens or dolphins and with masts erect amidships for sighting the fish, tossed up and down on the troubled waves. But few fishermen had gone out, for it was a bad day: they were sitting in the doorways of the houses at Ficarazzi, which are built all in rows, and playing cards. Gianni pointed them out to us.

"When they don't go out to sea, they all gamble," he said. "They gamble for misery."

Wagons and handcarts were passing along the road. B. wanted to photograph them all—those that carried straw and hay, or coal, or wood, or, since it was vintage time, grapes, or casks and barrels, or baskets of fruit or fish or vegetables, in fact the most varied assortment of things. There were also carts which were perambulating shops, containing all sorts of things, pots and pans and crockery and haberdashery. In some there were huge, brilliant pumpkins, cut and ready to be sold in slices to customers on the road, and purple and white eggplants stuck on sticks, like the heads of brigands displayed at the entrance to a village. As we came into Bagheria, we saw, at the sides of the road, a number of carts lying belly upward, with a complicated mass of carved pieces and tiny shapes painted white and yellow, like intestines laid out in the sun. These were carts under construction, and they were lying in front of the ancient shop of an old family of famous cart painters, the "Brothers Ducati, *late* Michele." On the door, which was encrusted with layer after layer of color like an abandoned palette, was written in English (the modern influence, perhaps): "Ducati Bros.—pictures"; but inside the entrance, where the brothers and their assistants worked, there was written up in large letters, standing out conspicuously on the opposite wall, the old-fashioned maxim: *Dio solo è grande,* God alone is great. We stopped to admire the skill with which an assistant was ornamenting a wheel and painting a

63

border on it, making it rotate beneath his brush, while one of the partners was busy painting, on an excellent oil-primed surface, a panel of a battle scene between Bradamante and Dama Rovenza, in splendid traditional colors, vermilion and yellow, green and blue. Inside the shop there were carriage doors and panels everywhere, and axle boxes with St. George engraved upon them, with iron fittings and arabesque patterns, and keys carved with the Infant Jesus, and shafts and crossbars—in fact, all the various parts of those wonderful vehicles that travel the roads of Sicily, fashioned and painted according to the precious designs handed down from father to son, of which there was a big chest full, in one corner. We left the painters and other craftsmen who were working in shops nearby, along the road, at carts and plows—carpenters, carvers, smiths and farriers—to go up the main street of Bagheria, which rises straight up from the sea, between the balconies of the houses, to the very top of the hill. B. wanted to see the monsters of the Villa Palagonia. He had heard so much about them that they were more or less of a disappointment; a strange row of grotesque statues. The eye becomes accustomed to grotesques of this sort at Palermo, where a stone face with a mustache or a beard, or grinding its teeth and grimacing, looks down from every archway. B. maintained that he had seen statues of exactly the same kind in China, on one of his journeys; and he discovered China again not only in these eighteenth century *chinoiseries* but in the villa itself, standing in its circular walled garden, and in its twisted trees. In the open space in front of the villa was pitched the tent of a traveling circus, and children were peeping through the cracks into its mysterious recesses. From that point one looks out over the sea, the Palermo sea on one side and the Cefalù sea on the other, with a mountain dividing them, behind which mountain live the fishermen of Aspra and the boat-builders of Porticello; and to the right rise the purple Madonia Mountains; and in front there is a brief expanse of plain covered with metallic green, almost black, orange groves, with isolated houses here and there, white, geometrical in design, with windowless walls and sharp, nervous structural angles. These sharp, nervous angles, these arid, violent colors, these relations of white and yellow and red, and of green and blue side by side (the colors of the carts), are the same as are to be found in the pictures of Guttuso, who was born here; and here (I thought to myself) one sees how true and faithful to the earth his painting is.

We stayed there for a short time, contemplating the green and blue expanse of earth and sea: but we had already idled about for too long, and the morning was almost gone. Hastening back over the road by which we had come, we left the coast at our backs, with the innumerable craftsmen and carters and peasants and fishermen who have been working there since time immemorial; and without stopping found ourselves back again at the gates of the town and took, at last, the inland road which leads to Lercara and Caltanisetta.

4

Of what awaited us at Lercara, and whether or not we should be able to visit the sulphur mines, we knew nothing. I had decided to go there merely because Lercara is the nearest mining area to Palermo, and because I had been advised to do so by one of the Sicilian gentlemen in whose company I had driven back from Isnello the evening before. He had told me that these sulphur mines were the most interesting I could possibly see, and that the greatest mining expert in all Sicily, Signor N., lived there—an old man without whose help no one could possibly understand anything about that subterranean world. No, he was not an engineer, he said, he had risen from the bottom, he was an old hand: for him alone the earth, the sulphur, the workmen, the tunnels held no secrets. He alone knew everything about it, and not an inch of ground would be dug up without him. The gentleman from Palermo told me that he himself was one of the owners of one of the mines in the area; that he knew old N. extremely well; and he had had the great kindness to give me one of his visiting cards to serve as an introduction for me to this wizard of the sulphur. He had heard (and I myself seemed to have seen something in the papers about it) that there had been a strike at Lercara, but he thought it was all over now: in any case it could only be, at the most, an attempted strike, or a partial strike, which would not interfere with my visit. It was just after this conversation that we had talked— as I have mentioned—about the Mafia, the Mafia that is a legend, an invention, the Mafia that does not exist. That was all I knew, except that Lercara Friddi was the native village of an illustrious "American," the famous Lucky Luciano, who had been sent back there by the American police, but who, according to what the newspapers say, prefers to live in peace and quiet in the isle of Capri. We were going, therefore, at a venture, to a place of which we knew nothing.

We had passed Misilmeri, we had gone up and down along the fine tree-lined road, and the mountain scenery of the interior was opening up in front of us. Climbing slowly, we reached the village of Bolognetta.

"Bolognetta, a little Bologna," observed B. "A little Bologna?" replied Gianni. "My goodness! It's a filthy little place. There isn't even any drainage: as a Palermitan, it makes me ashamed. Well, well," he added thoughtfully, "that's a thing for more important people than me to think about." The name of the village was not altogether new to me. I remembered having seen it in the reports of the Viterbo trial, the trial of Giuliano's band, on the occasion when the witness box had been occupied by a white-haired old man who had been arrested on a charge of associating, for criminal purposes, with one hundred and nine other persons; this was Serafino Di Peri, whose face, according to the reporter, was "formidable, like the face of the protagonist in a thriller film," and who had been, until 1948, the mayor of Bolognetta.

Beyond Bolognetta we entered regions which were unknown not only to B. and myself but also to our chauffeur, who had hardly ever been outside Palermo and had never come up as far as this; he was enjoying the novelty and the sense of discovery. He told us that he would like to emigrate, even if only to the mainland; life there was different; he was engaged to be married, but there was little work and he wanted to get away. But when we looked at these great stretches of land and the strange mountains rising in every direction, and spoke of their solemn beauty, Gianni's comment was: "You are right. We have our eyes full of outside things; our own things we don't see."

The old car became overheated on the hills; we had to stop every now and then to let it cool down. We had to halt a little way beyond Bolognetta. We got out and looked at the desolate scenery of the surrounding feudal estate, at the arid, treeless, deserted valleys. We walked a few steps into a field, on a steep slope: a forgotten donkey lying on the ground, and looking as though it had no legs, was the sole living creature in all that lonely expanse. But all of a sudden, from the bottom of the valley, a dog came running up to us, and after the dog, also running, a peasant, and after him another, older one and a boy, all coming to see who we were. When they reached us I asked whose this land was. "It's the property of the Conte San Marco," they said. "It's not all his now; he's sold some of it in little pieces. We rent about five acres." They had good manners, and were not mistrustful. In front of us, on the other side of the valley, in the direction of the invisible sea, the horizon was blocked by a high mountain. I asked if those were the Madonia Mountains, over there. "We call it the Montagna de Cane," said the old man. "We hear talk of the Madonie, we often hear talk of the Madonie, but we don't know where the Madonie are. All we know is the Montagna de Cane and Bolognetta."

We went on, beyond these changeless boundaries of the world. We left on our right-hand side the improbable pointed spur that hangs over Marineo, and penetrated into wide valleys and mountains ever more desolate, with distant villages perched on their sides; we passed beneath sheer rocks and into broad hollows where flocks of sheep, far away in the distance, were difficult to distinguish from stones; and the only human beings we came across were one or two shepherds, one or two carters and one or two road menders, naked to the waist, busy filling up holes. The silence of moon hung over these solitudes; ravens flew across the sky; earth was enfolded in the

69

noble austerity of the deserted landscape, as in a black mantle.

We had to stop again, for the sake of the car, at the entrance to the village of Vicari, which stands high on a hill with its earth-colored houses built against a strange-shaped whitish rock. Four black-clad women were sitting on a flight of steps, patiently awaiting the arrival of a bus which was due at goodness knows what time. A lame boy was hobbling quickly on his crutches up the steep street. A peasant on horseback was going down toward the fields, a plow like a long, prehistoric nail tied onto his saddle. Up above opens out an immense horizon of endless feudal estates over which the eye wanders as over a yellowish-gray sea. At the far edge of the fields, at the extreme boundary of the village, there was a placard on the end of a stick announcing: "Building land for sale." Who would want to build, I wondered, in these wastelands? However, a little farther up the road, we came upon a family of peasants busy building a house for themselves. They were all at work, men, women and children; they were digging trenches and carrying stones, while a couple of broken chairs and a table covered with tomato paste put out to dry waited in the wind—their first household goods—until the house should be ready. We had traveled very slowly, with many halts, and now we were late; it was almost three o'clock: but they told us we should find a better meal at Lercara than here at Vicari. Through open doors one could see into the peasants' houses, with their humble household utensils and bundles of sticks for the hearth, and babies in their mothers' arms. A little mangy, shaggy dog that looked like a hyena followed us howling. Under an archway some girls were almost buried under mountains of almonds, which they were cracking with hammers to be loaded into sacks. When they saw B., with his camera slung across his shoulders, staring at them in a way which was perhaps rather too indiscreet, they backed away from him, for fear of being photographed, and then began hurling insults and bad words at him; one of them took off a slipper and made as if to throw it at him. When we were back in the car, Gianni said: "They were afraid of losing their young men, if you took photographs of them."

The road led upward, into regions more and more deserted. We met no one—with the single exception of an ice cream seller on a motorcycle who rushed quickly past; who he was going to sell ices to, in those mountains, I do not know. There was a cold wind blowing, the sky was covered with gray clouds, and the sun had disappeared when, at a bend in the road, the village of Lercara Friddi became visible in the distance. With its squat houses, it lay spread out long and low on the ground, and to the left there was a wide, barren area, gray and yellowish, covered with little conical mounds of yellow debris: here were the mines. In a few minutes we were in the main street of Lercara; and as soon as we had got out of the car we realized that we had plunged into the heart of a battle and were in a village, as it were, in a state of siege.

Hundreds of carabineers, fully armed, filled the street; they were entering the shops, they were halted in trucks at the edge of the road, they were passing in groups, on patrol. The street was swarming with people; from every side we were bombarded with direct stares and with indirect, sidelong glances. There was a feeling of tension in the air, of a shared passion, as though all these people—what they were doing, one did not know—were moved by profound, important things, were awaiting grave and decisive events; and this gave an expression of keen watchfulness to all their faces.

This was no normal afternoon in a peasant village: it was a day of expectancy, as it might be in a town during a civil war. The strike was on, the first that had ever happened within the memory of man; and the life of each one of them was involved in it. I had come, out of simple curiosity, to visit an old sulphur mine at one of the thousand unchanging peasant villages; and I found myself, instead, in an active center, in full flood of change and movement, where all feelings were new, all actions passionate, all desires tense and violent, and where something that did not exist before was being born in the hearts of men.

My companions were tired and hungry. We had stopped, by chance, right in front of the only inn, an inn without a sign and, at that hour, without any customers. In any case there was nothing to eat, except cheese and eggs. Walking up and down the pavement, twenty paces one way and twenty paces back again, was a powerful young man with a cap placed insolently on the back of his head, a woolen pepper-and-salt suit of good quality, rather too short in the sleeves and trousers, a stupid, brutal face with a black thread of a mustache on the upper lip, an oblique, evasive way of looking at you, and a bearing which was at the same time arrogant and uneasy. If the Mafia (which does not exist) did exist, that, I thought to myself, is the typical, characteristic appearance of one of its members. He looked at our stationary car, examined it, walked away, retraced his steps. Other men like him, of similar repellent, violent, untrustworthy aspect, were walking up and down on the pavement opposite, or standing still, leaning against the walls of the houses, their hands in their pockets, their eyes watchful behind half-closed lids like shutters or the iron bars of a prison. Other men, in the clothes of the truly poor, were walking in the middle of the street or standing together in conversation.

It took a very long time for a couple of eggs to be got ready for us: the innkeeper and his family were eating their spaghetti amid clouds of flies, and were in no hurry. They did not give us many explanations about the strike: they did not know who we were. They said merely that the sulphur mine was occupied by the police, that the strike had been going on for more than a month, that the miners, who are paid at the end of the week's work, had been living so far on credit from the shopkeepers, but that, since it was the beginning of the month, they might perhaps present themselves for work again, being unable to pay their debts: and they said this in such a way that it was impossible for me to tell whether they desired or deprecated this surrender through starvation. But, partly from them, partly from a tobacconist, also from a carabineer and a passer-by, and even more from an old newspaper that I found on a table, I was able to discover, to some extent at least, what had happened.

From what I could gather putting two and two together, from these rapid, fragmentary pieces of evidence, the sulphur mines of the Lercara district, all of which are directed and, practically, owned by Signor N.—the Signor N. to whom I had been given an introduction—are old-fashioned and run by prehistoric methods. There are no adequate safety measures; the work is carried on under very hard conditions; there are women and boys working there as well; and wages are far below the minimum established by general contract. Everything went on under conditions of the most absolute immutability: days and years followed each other unvaryingly, since nothing is more stable, more sure, more unmoving than a feudal regime. Until three months before there had been no trade union organization: it had seemed that the resignation of the poor would last for ever. But on June 18th a boy of eighteen working in the mine, Michele Felice by name, had been crushed by a fall of rock in one of the tunnels and killed. It is a thing that often happens: the dead boy's father, too, had had a leg crushed by a fall of rock in the mine. In the boy's pay envelope part of his wages had been deducted, because, owing to his death, he had not finished his day's work; and all five hundred miners had been docked an hour's pay—the hour during which they had interrupted their work in order to dig him out and bring him up to the light, from the bottom of the mine. An ancient sense of justice was aroused: the despair of centuries found, in this act, a visible symbol, and the strike began. It lasted for twenty days, then it stopped, then began again, after retaliatory dismissals, accompanied, now, by precise union demands on the subject of wages, insurance, safety measures, freedom of organization; and it still continued, nor was it possible to foresee how it would end.

Having obtained this scanty amount of news, we came out of the inn and asked where Signor N. was to be found. He was only a few steps away, in his office, which opened onto the street, onto the same pavement upon which we were standing, where the men whom I had noticed on our arrival still went on walking up and down, uneasily watching.

It was a sort of warehouse, divided by a partition into two, an entrance lobby and an office, with a small table and a few chairs and bare walls. In the lobby sat an old man, gigantic in size, heavy, coarse, with a short, strong neck, wearing an open shirt and a shabby gray coat; the skin on the top of his head was like leather, he had enormous jaws, a mouth full of teeth and sly, evasive eyes behind the thick lenses of a pair of iron spectacles. This was Signor N., the excise officer and owner of the mines. But how can one describe him? Perhaps only a painting could give the expression of that countenance, the atmosphere that enveloped it, the unusual manner in which it moved. It was an impassive, impenetrable face, but at the same time it moved in grimaces that expressed feelings different from those which we are accustomed to understanding: a mixture of astuteness, extreme mistrust, assurance mingled with fear, arrogance and violence and possibly even a certain measure of wit: but all these things seemed to be fused, in that face, in a manner that, for us, was remote and strange, as though the tone of the feelings and the very appearance of the face belonged to another period, a period of which we retain merely an archaic hereditary memory.

I had a vivid impression that I was in the company of a rare representative of a lost race, of a man not of today, nor of yesterday, nor of a hundred years ago, but one of those who lived a thousand years back, in that period of the world which has left scarcely any documents and which we can only imagine. He received us with extreme suspicion. We should not be able to visit the mines, he said: they were occupied by the police: not even he himself could get in. He was not interested in who I was: if I wrote books, he had never heard of them. The card of introduction which I had given him and which he turned round and round contemptuously in his hands, meant nothing to him: he did not remember who the gentleman was: certainly he was not a mineowner, he had never known him, either personally or by name. If, as I said, I had come to see the sulphur mines, I might go back home again. To calm him down, the best I could do was to praise a big picture hanging on the lobby wall (a daub by a local artist, a certain Gattuso, representing, in fact, the exterior of one of the mines), and, finally, his own face, which was quite worthy of a picture, or at least a photograph. "Me—a photograph?" he exclaimed. "That's forbidden, absolutely forbidden. Nobody has ever taken one of me, nor will they ever do so. The doctor has forbidden it," he added with a smile that displayed a formidable row of teeth, "and the chemist too." As he said this he noticed that B. had his apparatus across his shoulders, all ready for use; and, so as to be quite certain of not being photographed, Signor N. rose up, big and heavy as a rock, from his chair, and leaned, back to back, against B.: in this way he could not be taken by surprise. In the meantime two young men who were Signor N.'s sons had come in and were standing in the doorway, and others with them, both young and old: I don't know who they were. I told him he must be careful, photographers are devils, capable of anything: and in the meantime B., who, though smaller, is also sturdy and strong, was gradually moving and turning round on his own axis. Signor N. followed his movements, slowly pirouetting, and kept carefully back to back with him, so that in a short time they found themselves rotating in the middle of the room, in a kind of cautious, very slow dance, like a miming ballet representing Mistrust. Then B. was extremely clever. At a certain moment he let off a sudden flash into the air: Signor N., taken

77

by surprise, took a step backward, and B. took advantage of this to launch—like a Jupiter of photography —a second lightning flash, and to take a photograph of him, saying, however, that it was only a joke and that there was no film in the camera. "I got Churchill like that, in the bath," he said; and Signor N. seemed to be amused by the jest and the comparison, and, becoming apparently more cordial, took us into his office and made us sit down in front of his desk. Here he repeated that he could not arrange for us to see the mine, which in any case was empty and at a standstill, but that if we liked we might try and procure an authorization from the chief of police. The strike? That would soon be over: the workmen had no money to pay their debts. It was a political question, a political strike. And he remembered now who the gentleman was who had given me his visiting card; yes, Don Nicola, one of the owners of a mine in the district. If I was a writer, I ought to read a little book which had been written against him, and tell him what I thought of it. It was nothing but lies and unbelievable enormities. He called one of his sons, told him to get me a copy of it, to give me a cup of coffee and to show me the road leading to the sulphur mines.

The son led us to the café, with a hundred eyes following us, and told the keeper of the café to find a copy of the pamphlet for me. But both B. and I had the impression, whether rightly or wrongly, that, as he asked him to get it, he gave him a wink and a stealthy sign with his hand to tell him not to. In the end he made us promise that we would come back and fetch it at the office; and we got into the car and drove off. We went through streets of low houses, passed in front of the church, into the miners' quarter, then came out of the village and at once found ourselves facing the mines. At this point the young man said he must go back home, and hastily ran off.

We were left there, B. and I, staring at the deserted waste. Below us, in the last light of day, peasants were coming back along the path from the fields, with their donkeys and goats, turning their heads neither to right nor left. But in front of us silence and solitude lay heavy over the mounds of debris, the sulphur-yellow soil, the tottering, cracked chimneys like ruined towers. A last streak of pink and purple and violet appeared in the cold, gray sunset sky above the infernal yellow of the earth. Then, from behind one of the evil-looking mounds there leaped forth a man dressed in black, with a gun over his arm, and, running as if to attack us, raced down toward us. Behind him appeared five carabineers in battle dress, and followed him, at a run, with their tommy guns; they immediately surrounded us and called to us to halt where we were. The man in black was one of Signor N.'s sworn guards: he could not let us pass, he told us, without a stamped permit from Signor N. or unless he was present in person: only if Signor N. authorized it could we go in: our word was not enough. The five carabineers with their unbelievable black mustaches were even worse disposed toward us and seemed anxious to make the most thorough possible examination of us—in a malevolent manner, too; but a great display of eloquence, if it did not suffice to get us one single step farther, at least caused us to be allowed to turn back without further annoyance or injury.

We went off, therefore, toward the village, in the oncoming darkness. Before we reached the houses, a man jumped out from the shadows and thrust two copies of the pamphlet at me through the lowered window of the car. "Take it and read it," he said, running behind the car as we went on. The pamphlet was entitled "The Challenge of the Sulphur Mines—Letter from Lercara Friddi, by Mario Farinella": it was the one that Signor N. had promised me: yet it did not seem to me that the man who gave it to me, or his impassioned voice, came from *that* direction.

At the entrance to the village there was a great crowd awaiting us: men, women and children blocked the street with arms interlocked, and surrounded the car as soon as it stopped. These were the miners. "Who are you?" they shouted. "Have you been to the mine? Who sent you?" The women, with babies in their arms, seemed the most ruthless and even menacing. I got out and told them who I was, and that I was a friend. Someone knew about me, and their faces and accents changed immediately. "But why did you go to N.? Why didn't you come to us?" they asked. They apologized for having taken me for an emissary or an agent of the excise officer: one of them had been following me all the afternoon, not knowing who I was: he had seen me drinking coffee with Signor N.'s son and then go to the sulphur mines, upon which they too had placed an embargo. So they had sent out a summons and had mustered together to stop me; they had thought ill of me and now were glad they had been mistaken. The copies of the pamphlet had been brought to me by one of them who had been in the café and had also seen young N.'s gesture of contradiction, and had then run off to procure them for me. How instantly they had changed, those angry, hostile faces which I now saw round me, in the gloom, shining with confidence and cheerful friendliness! They asked me to go with them, saying they would tell me everything there was to be told about the mine; they wanted me to hear it all and to talk about it. I promised to join them later: first I wished to go back to Signor N.'s office, as I had promised him.

Signor N. welcomed me, this time, with a wide and beaming smile, a smile which grew even wider when I told him that first the *carabinieri* had wanted to arrest me and then the miners to beat me. He was seated in the midst of a court of friends and followers who were standing all round the walls, and I suspected—wrongly perhaps—that this fact of my meeting with some trouble or other had been his desire, or his hoped-for amusement, in sending me on my way to the mine. He said, as I had foreseen, that he could not give me a copy of the pamphlet (I touched the two copies I had in my pocket); he had found one copy, with great difficulty, but he needed that in order to take action against the author. But I might have a quick glance at it now. "Just think," he said, "they call me 'Nero!' And they call my wife 'Donna Rachele.' And look at this, what nonsense—would you believe it possible? To say that Donna Rachele remarked: 'I'll paper the rooms with banknotes rather than increase your wages!' And that I sacked the accountant because his wife didn't give up her seat in church to me; and that I sacked a miner, Schillati, because he had gone to take his dead daughter's body to the cemetery; and a whole lot of other enormities! Look, he calls me the terrible N., the slave driver who is an offense to the whole of Sicily. Ha, ha!" and he began to laugh, showing all his teeth. I looked hastily at the pamphlet: here was a description of the appalling life in the mine, the starvation wages, the deaths of miners, the feudal conditions at Lercara—a true story. There was mention of the whips that were used to make boys of ten to thirteen work in the pits, of the acts that amazed and amused Signor N., and of many others. I do not know whether they were all true: but faces speak for themselves by their looks and expressions; and as I listened and looked at the faces that surrounded me in that warehouse, it seemed to me that these stories might all be credible.

Outside, in front of the café, I encountered a tall, well-dressed man, who greeted me and said he had read my books. He was a gentleman of the neighborhood, a liberal, he said, and a supporter of self-government for Sicily. "You have arrived at a bad moment," he said. "The strike is on, and the miners are going hungry. Certainly Signor N. has his faults, but not in the way you may perhaps think. Life is difficult for the mineowners too. The people who are really responsible are not here, they are in Rome. It's the Sulphur Board: we have to hand over the sulphur at thirty and they resell it at eighty: and it's those bureaucrats who squander the difference. Believe me, Rome is eating us up, all of us Sicilians."

In the darkness, which was now complete, old and young men were awaiting me at the corners of the streets to show me the way to the street where the "Michele Felice Miners' League" had its headquarters. First one, then two, then three, and finally ten of them were escorting B. and me, in silence, through the black lanes, and in the thick darkness I could not see their faces. The headquarters of the league, situated in a narrow alley, was a big room full of benches upon which sat women suckling babies, and children and old people, and in the middle and all round there was a dense crowd of men; and they all applauded, clapping their hands in sign of friendship and good understanding when we came in. They told me their stories, the evils they had to endure, the hunger, the tyrannies, the hardships—the whole life of the poverty-stricken sulphur miner. But that was not what counted, either for them or for me, at the moment. When they spoke of their misfortunes, their eyes and their expressions were cheerful, open and smiling. They were thin, some of them disfigured by accidents, and many of them, both children and men, bore on their faces the signs of

disease, of tuberculosis and prolonged undernourish‚
ment. But it seemed as though they had all of them
forgotten these things, moved by a flood of enthusiasm
for what was happening, for what they were doing,
all of them together, all of them in unison. They
were proud, and sure of victory, and happy to have
discovered themselves as human beings and free
men, happy with a new kind of happiness which
showed itself in the expression, both touched and
touching, on all their faces. They were new faces,
faces of today, eyes which, today, saw things that until yesterday had been hidden, eyes which saw themselves. Fundamentally, I said to myself, this is nothing but an ordinary, normal episode of social struggle, identical with thousands of others that took place
everywhere a hundred years ago, in England, in
France, all over Europe, even in Italy. Only we are no
longer a hundred years ago, we are in the year 1951;
and the face of Signor N., against whom they are
struggling, belongs not to a hundred, but to a thousand, years ago; it is not the face of an English indus-
trialist of 1848, but possibly that of a slaveowner of
the eighth or ninth century, before the year 1000,
and possibly not even that; and they too, these people who are now glowing with new-found life, were,
until yesterday, the slaves of some remote period.
And the pleasure they have at feeling themselves
alive, and their sureness of victory, derive from an
ineffable, unconscious sense of having undertaken a
role in a real adventure, of having plunged into the
moving stream of history. None of them would ever

say to me: "We don't know where the Madonia Mountains are: all we know is the Montagna de Cane and Bolognetta (or Lercara and the sulphur mine)." They spoke as though the whole world were open to them, as though there were no more secrets or limits. And they spoke without anger, and in courteous tones, even of N. They felt themselves to be no longer alone.

Upon the wall at the far end of the room there hung a portrait of the dead boy, Michele Felice: there were no party devices nor portraits of politicians: the picture of the dead boy was the only one. Underneath it was a small crucifix, and there was another, larger crucifix to one side. They looked at the portrait of their dead comrade with eyes of enthusiasm and almost of gratitude. It was from there that life, for them, and the feeling of being alive, had originated. I could not help reflecting that these men, who had spent their days below ground, like the dead, in the sulphurous material hell of the dead, were now experiencing their own resurrection. They were well contented, all of them: the old women, the women feeding their babies, the young men, the tall, very handsome Drago, secretary of the league, who was their leader: it was as though they had been born yesterday. They all wanted to be photographed: they had found the courage to exist, and were no longer enemies of their own semblances. B. satisfied them. When he wished to take a photograph of the wall with the portrait of Michele Felice, one of the miners, with the ingenuous zeal of a neophyte, made

85

as if to remove the crucifixes. I begged him to leave them.

It was getting late, and we had to go. Many of them accompanied us, through the dark lanes, to the car; and we shook hands cheerfully.

We drove through the darkness, with feeble, faint headlights, over the black expanses of the feudal estates. A polecat ran swiftly across the road. Gianni, who did not know what to think of what he had seen at Lercara, broke the silence, after some time, to say, in his childish sort of way: "That Signor N. has a face just like Canimanza" (he meant Gano di Maganza). And then he began telling stories of the paladins, of cross-eyed Roland, of Rinaldo the leader of the forty thieves, of Madama Roversa, the enchanted Saracen, who could be killed only by the sword of Roland, and only if struck in one particular place, and that the most intimate and secret and feminine; and of how Rinaldo killed her, after stealing —as was his custom—Roland's sword, and then lying down among the dead and transfixing the Amazon in exactly the right spot, from below upward, as she went past. But the lights of Palermo were already twinkling in the distance, and we came down to the blessed, seaweed-scented coast.

5

Night had fallen, and the city below us was brilliant
with lights; the sea was a jet-black plain, shut in by
the barren mass of Monte Pellegrino, like a side
scene in a theater, glimmering white in the darkness
as though made of calcined bone. My friend B. was
determined to see the cemetery of the Capuchin
monks (he had to leave very early next morning);
but we did not know whether it would be possible
at that hour. So we almost flew through the suburbs
and streets of Palermo; and, turning aside swiftly
through dim side streets toward the Porta Nuova,
among people who were going into the humble shops
to make their last purchases of sugar paladins for
All Saints' Day on the morrow, we drove up the
avenue of cypresses and quickly found ourselves in
front of the ancient monastery.

The door, naturally, was closed. A young, bearded
monk opened it to us, mistook us for foreigners, in
whom any sort of oddity is tolerable, and resigned

himself, after many insistences and prayers on our side, to accompanying us with a candle into the dark vaults. But we must make haste, he said, because he had to come up again for supper and for his devotions: just a quick glance, then, to satisfy us. We should see very little by that small, flickering light: the electric lighting did not go beyond the staircase that led down underground: we should have to come back by daylight if we wanted to see more, when the light filters in through the high, narrow windows at street level. And so we went down the staircase toward the dense blackness of the catacombs, and walked forward into them, hesitatingly at first, on the uneven floor, in the tenuous circle of candlelight which made the darkness that enfolded us on every side even more profound and mysterious. We made our way through corridors that were lost in blackness and that seemed limitless; and then suddenly, issuing unexpectedly from the gloom, in endless rows, on both sides, the dead were with us.

The first to come into our circle of vision against the gray walls as soon as our eyes had become accustomed to the feeble yellowish light that seemed to make the darkness thicker were little more than skeletons, their skulls covered with faded, wasted skin; yet it was still possible to see, from their cast of expression, and even more from their hair and habits, that they had been monks. We wanted to stop and look at these first ones, but the monk, who was in a hurry, went on with his candle along the corridors, telling us that we should see finer and better preserved ones farther on. And indeed, among the interminable crowd of nameless skeletons, ready, as it were, in their dried-up equality, for an egalitarian last judgment, there now emerged, here and there against the walls, a few well-preserved faces, with hair and beards and a frozen energy of movement, faces in which one looked, almost, for the brightness of a glance beneath the concealing arches of the eyebrows. Our guide raised the candle in their direction, causing the shadows to move as he moved his hand; and as some of them were bending forward or askew or threatening to fall, he corrected their positions with the quick, familiar gesture of one who, being accustomed to this company of dead men, no longer felt either its fascination or its terror; or, even more, like the keeper of a shop where they sell dolls, or marionettes for a puppet theater—those deceitful images of heroes and of men. He told us the story of this one or that, and of the old church of the Madonna della Pace or the Madonna di Mezzo Agosto, which was almost destroyed when Admiral Ottavio d'Aragona had it reconstructed in 1621; and of how these catacombs, the ancient burying place of the people of Palermo, had existed since the year 1559, or perhaps even earlier. The dead were buried here in graves (the floor upon which we were walking was simply a pavement of tombstones fitted in among disconnected bricks); but the richer ones, or those who wished it, were embalmed; and it was they who formed the multitude of dead who were looking at us from every side. This practice had lasted until

1881, when it was forbidden by law, actually before the time when the Madonna di Mezzo Agosto came to be occupied (in 1898) by the Capuchins, who had founded there the International College of Foreign Missions and a famous library of Arab collections and of texts of Greek and Latin orators. There are still today about eight thousand complete mummies, besides the dead who are buried and those who have vanished. They are divided roughly into four groups —priests, women, illustrious men and ordinary people; there is a separate group of noblemen; but these divisions are not strict, owing to the mixing of different periods, to family regroupings, and to children being placed here and there, all over the place.

Almost all the dead men are standing upright against the walls, in one or two rows; many are fully dressed, in clothes that are wasted and motheaten and gray with time and dust; others are enveloped in plain nightshirts or shrouds, and many of them have lost these coverings and stand there with their bodies wrapped merely in sackcloth, a last humble, wrinkled skin beneath which ribs and bones are visible. The women are all lying down; young girls and virgins have crowns and palm leaves. Much damage was done to the dead during recent years, the young monk told us; the air raids shook the monastery, cracked the glass of the windows and broke the urns, knocked over many of the dead who were standing against the walls, so that some of them lost arms or heads or feet: it was a big job putting them back in place. More and more new figures, new gestures, new individuals full of a character eternal and for ever fixed, kept issuing from the gloom. In order to enlighten us about the mystery of this lasting quality, this preservation of dead bodies even without the secret balsams of Egypt and even when left exposed to the air without protection, the monk showed us some small rooms without any openings, the so-called *sgocciolatoi* or draining rooms, which, in their shape and also because of certain slabs of striated stone intersected by cracks, reminded me of similar places at the Cerveteri and in the Etruscan cemeteries. Here, he explained, corpses were thrown down and left to dry in the moistureless air of the closed room, for a year; by which time all the humors, all the fluids, had drained away and the dried, immutable image was ready to take its place among the crowd of the dead.

Whether the procedure for embalming was as simple as this, or, as I had read some time before, more complicated, I do not know. Possibly the dead were embalmed with herbs, after the stomach had been opened and the entrails removed; and immersed before they were hung up to dry, in a bath of lemon; then, after the drying process was finished, filled with straw, dressed again in their own clothes and carried into the catacombs. There may also have been another more refined and more expensive method, by which the dead were preserved, after embalming, in sealed glass cases. Certainly whichever of these methods was used, this multitude of dead persons is now at a standstill in time; and the slow change and decay of these hardened skins, worm-eaten and covered with dust, seems merely to accentuate the character of individual lives, of individual stories fully told in features that have become, in their immobility, quintessential. The hurrying monk had shown us the best preserved: a bishop, a surgeon, a priest, some little girls, an American consul with a big black mustache and a picture of Santa Rosalia on his chest, who had been placed here, as a special concession, in 1911, many years after it had been forbidden; and a young girl of marvelous grace and naturalness who looked as though she were asleep and breathing in her crystal casket, beneath the sheet of glass all covered with drops of wax, with a ribbon in her hair which appeared just faintly moist and her fine lashes edging her closed lids. She too had arrived by special concession of the government, as lately as 1920: she was the youngest, the most recent, the most intact of all the dead.

We had reached a place where the corridors intersected, and where, in an open case, lay a man with long black hair and the romantic mustaches and beard of the Risorgimento period, one of Garibaldi's generals, Giovanni Corrao, who was murdered in the Palermo revolt of 1863. Among the white linen folds of his shroud, this idealistic, resolute face, this Garibaldian beard, were far more alive than a history book, and by their physical presence revived, for our eyes, a period which has already become only a memory. Here B. took out his camera and other implements: the monk made no objection to his taking photographs, but said that he himself must go up again and that he would leave us here by ourselves, provided we did not stay long. B. accompanied him as far as the stairs with the candle, and I stayed waiting for him in the darkness, beside the Garibaldi general.

It was a long way through the labyrinth of passages, and B. took a long time to come back. I started lighting matches and looking around me by their fugitive light. Not far from me, in a side corridor, were two little girls who seemed to be moving forward out of their niche, and all around them were many other little girls in attitudes like living people who have been smitten by some common misfortune; it was as though they were all breathing still, yet their faces had gone gray, their hair and clothes had lost their color, through some pestilence. "It came down through one of those doors . . .": this phrase regarding the plague and the expectation of death came into my mind as I looked at these little sisters, who had died in 1860 through the collapse of their home, and who seemed ready now to fall from this their last threshold, in their simple finery and with ribbons on their childish clothes. But now, at the far end of the corridor, appeared B.'s candle and the brilliant flash of his magnesium lamp.

Together we made the long circuit again, stopping to converse with the dead. Here were priests and monks with ropes round their necks, their heads bowed in humility or upturned to heaven in a gesture of protest; here crowned virgins and babies, the smallest of them, in her little cap, only two and a half months old; and below her the little daughter of a rich merchant, dressed like an old lady; here, three great lawyers of the Palermo bar, fiercely gnashing their teeth between the Mafia and the law; and Concettina, ten years old, "dear loving little angel," as she is described on the scroll pinned to her dress; here, in a corridor full of ordinary people, was a man before whom other heads fell, looking as if he had just risen from a savage meal in the uttermost depths of hell; here, some ascetic priests, fanatical, preaching; and an enormous bishop wearing a curious miter of worked silk, a spectacular figure with a peculiarly ferocious kind of fatness, with heavy eyelids and cheeks and a worm-eaten chin, still swollen with an altogether earthly greed and attached to this life of ours as no living man can be; and here was Ignazio Sanfilippo, professor of political economy, reduced to sheer skeleton yet still professorial and learned (beside him an unknown corpse, with long, scanty hair and an unshaven beard looking as if it had grown after death, recalled the living dead in the concentration camps of Buchenwald and Belsen).

In a torn, discolored but still impressive gown, a great lawyer with a high, prominent forehead goes haranguing down into eternity, and Professor Salvatore Manzella, a famous surgeon, is clothed in a white doctor's tunic sewn up with long stitches of twine over the chest, as though he had stitched himself up for the last operation. There they all stand, like living people, drained of the temporary, of the

uncertain qualities of life, their personal characteristics enhanced. B. was taking flashlight photographs;
and, since he had recently returned from America,
he was telling me of the cemeteries there and of the
embalming processes which are carried out with the
intention of concealing death. He had in his pocket
the advertisement-catalogue of one of these cemeteries: furniture, carpets, invisible music, hairdress-
ing, lacquering, makeup, paint for the dead whose
death must never show. Here, in this ancient land,
it is exactly the opposite. Death is death, and since
it is death it preserves in itself, fully, the image of
life.

In other parts of Italy, and in Rome too, there
are cemeteries of this kind; but here, in Sicily, this
familiarity with the dead, their continuing presence,
seem more natural and awaken no terror; so that I
do not believe in the truth of the legend that is told
about the caretaker of a cemetery who went mad because he saw a skull running along by itself and roll-
ing about on the floor because there was a mouse
shut up inside it. There are other cemeteries of the
kind in Sicily, such as the Cappuccinelle, an aristo-
cratic convent where some twenty noble ladies stand,
elegantly dressed, in niches in a square room, their
heads wrapped in lace coifs. In the church at Gangi,
Mass is said among the priests of the village, who,
ever since the seventeenth century, have been embalmed and plunged in wax and are forever present
at the religious ceremonies. But in no place so much
as here at Palermo is there an entire population of

the dead, with all the variety of a population and its customs and a sort of silent understanding and seriousness. Each one has his own individual face and character, but there is something which is common to all of them, a particular shade of expression, the image, perhaps, of the death's-head which, as the Roman poet says, is contained in the head of every one of the living. There is something common to all that grayness, in that worn look, which strangely resembles the look that is common to the faces of the poor: and that thing is death, which is one short step beyond misery; death which, like misery, even more than misery, gives to all faces a look of truth.

We noticed suddenly that the candle was almost finished. Its last drops of wax were already falling hot upon my fingers: so as not to be left in the dark we hastened as quickly as we could toward the staircase. At the top we found the young monk waiting for us. B. was embarrassed as to whether or not he would accept a tip. Blushing and holding out five hundred lire, he said: "For your poor people, father." The Capuchin suffered from no such embarrassment. He looked at the banknote with an air of contempt and said: "Aren't you even going to pay me for the candle?" B. doubled his offering and we left him still discontented.

TWO

1

On my right, in the direction of the sea, the moon was shining, big and round, over the fields of Nicotera, gray in the hour before dawn, and already, on the other side, behind the mountains of Calabria, the sky was clearing and vague clouds were drawing together and taking shape in the clear, transparent heavens. As soon as I awoke, I looked through the narrow window frame in the moving train at this moon gleaming in the liquid violet-gray metal of the sky, wondering, almost, whether it might not be a sun gone pale; and saw too, passing close to me, silver woods and fields of orange and lemon trees with cool, dark shadows and globes of fruit phosphorescent with an interior red and yellow light of their own, like a thousand little suns. Slow pillars of smoke rose on unknown distant hills; silence enfolded the deserted countryside, the nameless torrent beds, the rocks, the beaches, the sea, the marvelous olive trees, the mysterious breathing of this unknown coast, of this last coast of Italy before the Straits and fabulous Sicily.

The *Secondo Aspromonte,* the ferry-ship, received the carriages of our train on board, ready to cast off. Sitting on boxes, women with wide white and blue skirts that hung in folds knitted steadily, without raising their eyes to look at the trains, as calm, in the early morning hour, as if this work of theirs had been going on forever without pause. Other young women were sitting on the floor among sacks and baskets, the bright folds of their wide skirts flowing about them, silent and still, in languid, harmonious attitudes. People got out of the railway carriages and went up on the deck. We waited for a little train that could be seen approaching along the coast from Reggio; and then the crowd arrived, running—boy students and fair-haired girl students, smart, well-dressed clerks, and finally, all alone, an old woman in peasant costume, a white handkerchief with red ribbons on her head, and a white and blue and pink cotton dress. In the saloons and on the decks young men with fine, bright-colored scarves round their necks sat languidly about, turning their big dark eyes hither and thither. A gipsy woman was moving around among the various groups, she wore a sulphur-yellow scarf on her head, an orange blouse, a pink skirt and iron-gray stockings, and looked like some strange, brilliant flower. Young banana sellers went past hawking their wares. "Do you want some bananas? I have a very fine bunch," whispered one of these boys in my ear, smiling as he reclined his head gently on his shoulder and speaking in a tone of extreme courtesy—that Sicilian courtesy which is to be found in the manners, the faces, the words of everyone.

After we left, we met and passed the *Scilla*, the ferry-ship coming from Messina—white like ours, with tricolor funnels, red-painted ventilators, flags unfurled: they are most elegant ships, decked out for their daily work as though for a *festa*. At first the people on the decks of our ship were silent, perhaps because of the early hour; then suddenly their voices burst forth, all at the same time, in a curious clamor, voices which, from the very first moment of being heard, were loud, without modulation, exaggerated, as though the words that each person was saying were the last of his life. Above this continuous clamor fragments of their remarks floated forth, logical modes of expression unusual in the ordinary speech of other parts of Italy, the logical connecting links in a judicious and naturally complex way of thought, a popular inheritance from ancient Greek clarity. We were now in the middle of the Straits, and a beautifully framed placard declared: "Notice to passengers. Anyone seeing a person fall into the sea must shout 'man overboard,' and anyone hearing the shout 'man overboard' must repeat it and must try to see that it reaches the bridge as soon as possible." Thus, with bureaucratic politeness, are we defended from the mythological monsters, Scylla and Charybdis. Villa San Giovanni was now at our backs, gray and pink on its low hill; in front of us Messina was almost invisible in the shadow of the clouds, and only the point of Capo Faro gleamed in the early sunshine. The sun was rising behind the mists over Mt. Aspromonte, Etna was covered with rain-swollen clouds, Italy and the mainland receded amid flying throngs of seagulls; and now Messina was opening out in front of us beneath its confused network of hills, delicate, ethereal in the clear air, the valleys strewn with mist. A sound of bugles reached us from the distant barracks. The outline of churches and houses, and of the campanile containing the famous clock with the lion and the cock, repeated, along the shore, the strange jagged pattern of the mountains.

And now our train was running along the coast of the Ionian Sea, toward the ancient cities and the volcano. There were fishermen at sea, others sitting on the beaches working at their nets, and boats were drawn up all along beside the railway. The houses of villages huddled under the dark hill covered with prickly pear. Children climbed on the railings to watch the train pass, and old women muffled in shawls watched it from behind windowpanes. Peasants were stooping in the market gardens, in groups, and there were men and women in the citrus plantations, calm, slow in their movements, dressed in rags of wonderful colors. Little boys went past, sitting erect, silent, confident, in carts drawn by betasseled horses. We crossed immensely wide river beds, expanses of stones over which the carts pass; rocks, reefs, small islands jutted jaggedly from the sea; a high mountain, abrupt, yellowish in color, rose up: and we were at Taormina. It is one of the most

102

famous places in the world, yet its fame does not contrive to spoil it; nor do big hotels, nor tourists, nor night clubs, nor men of letters, nor the dubious international society which collects there and which becomes even more vulgar in the midst of that austere, archaic nature, nor yet the cheap but celebrated follies of its curious guests. This volcanic air, this shining sea seem to enfold everything impassively and to enforce a harmonious contemplation even upon the most insensitive and the most crazy. I once looked down from the top of the Greek theater upon the steep, deserted countryside: there was a market gardener, very small in the distance, standing, spade in hand, in his little field, and there beside him was his young wife holding a baby in her arms. I followed them with my eyes for a long time: they were one with the earth and the landscape and the sea. They stood still, looking round, then took a few steps and stopped again, with gestures that were ancient and exactly right, forgetful for the moment of work and spade and furrow, as though their task were simply to look and be looked at.

On the other side of the town, beyond the Capuchin monastery, at the "Fontana Vecchia," lived D. H. Lawrence, and from there he left for his journey to Sardinia, fleeing from demonic Etna and the demonic Sicilians of Etna, strange creatures, according to him, intelligent and without souls. A few people still remember him as one of a large number of bizarre Englishmen who have pitched their tents in this eternal landscape. The landlady of his house, with an air of boredom at having been questioned altogether too often about him, had a vague memory of him. "There are two Germans here now, and they're writers too." In the garden there is a tree with strange fruit, green and wrinkled, like a marine pumice stone. *"Pane d'India*—bread of India—my husband calls it," she told me. Workmen building a house in the open country were singing "Ridi pagliaccio" transformed into an Arab chant. In the ruined church of San Domenico, near the splendid hotel, the statue of a warrior in armor, leaning on his right arm as he sleeps, with his great sword at his side, lies among the rubble beside a wall. Women pass along the roads, broad-faced, their hair dressed like crowns, and with large, long eyes, like archaic statues; and behind the houses and trees and rocks rise Mount Etna, blue, snow-covered.

But Taormina, the jeweled gate of Sicily and the Ionian Sea, was now left behind, and the train was moving along the coast again, the Greek coast of fishermen and peasants. At Giardini almost all the doors bear mourning ribbons, many of them whitened by the sun of the years that have passed, with printed legends upon them: "For my husband," "For my mother," "For my father," "For my wife," "For my son," and so on. Even on the door of Giardini station there was a mourning ribbon—for the relation of some railwayman, perhaps. The fields now were full of people at work, women picking olives, peasants and boys in the citrus plantations, and they seem like a happy people, full of elegance and grace. But all of a sudden this paradise of green and gold is cut across by a great black stripe like an immense mourning ribbon laid on the earth; this is the great *sciara* of Mascali, the expanse of petrified lava which in 1928 came down from the distant crater all the way to the sea, submerging the village beneath its black and fiery wave. Mascali has now been rebuilt lower down, immediately below the high wall of basalt where laborers work to split the stone and to open ways through. Above, in the direction of the mountain, as far as the eye can reach, stretches the black disorder of an aboriginal, newborn nature, the petrified smoke of the white-hot bowels of the world, a black, undulating sea, wrinkled, shriveled, begrimed, the dark milk of Etna's breast which has flowed down in sooty streams into the defenseless green of the countryside. These fleeting pictures, however, were soon replaced by the noble churches of Acireale, the curved beach of Aci Trezza covered with painted boats, the rocks of the Cyclops hurled by Etna-Polyphemus into the sea, the castle of Aci erect and black on its great basalt rock. And now we were coming into the black suburbs of Catania, between the houses of Ognina which is built upon the congealed smoke of a tempest of lava, and here we were in black, smoke-built Catania itself. At the station we got into an old, ramshackle carriage, with worn black leather seats and a black, closed hood, which was drawn at great speed by an old black horse; and through long, straight, smoky, working-class streets came out at last into the center of the town, among the marvels of the eighteenth century's most beautiful city.

It was early evening; the Via Etnea was filled with an innumerable crowd of people, as if the town contained not merely its own three hundred thousand inhabitants, but a million, or two million others as well, or even more, and they had all come out into this particular street to look at each other, to examine each other, to converse in the half-darkness. The streets are as dark as if the wartime blackout were still going on, thanks, they told me, to the monopoly of the local electricity company. But one gets accustomed to this darkness, and Vaccarini's architecture shows up all the better for it in the moonlight. The Via dei Crociferi, at night, has a mysterious enchantment, what with its churches and its arch, even if the headless horse no longer prowls about it, as in the nights of the eighteenth century. The Castello Ursino gazes at the sea from which the lava has separated it, the black, unfinished tower of the Benedictines looks even blacker against the black sky as it rises above its great façade. Stone elephants adorn the piazzas and the places, bearing on their backs the initial of the saint. Saint Agatha, indeed, is depicted everywhere, and a fierce executioner tears off her breast with pincers.

A crowd of young men, friends old and new, growing ever more numerous, now accompanied me— every one of them full of an extreme, a genuine courtesy combined with a great enjoyment of conversation, and the Greek clarity, the Greek sophistry.

We wandered around streets and cafés, looking at people, analyzing characters; this love of dividing people into types is one of the chief tendencies of the Hellenistic spirit here in Catania. There are some, it seems, who spend their time creating types in reality, influencing and fashioning some chosen victim according to a plan of their own, for the sole pleasure of being able to give a detailed description of him, like those seventeenth-century painters whose sketches of pictures previously executed in sculpture are preserved in the museum. We talked of the saint, of her savage feast day, of the sweetmeats made by the nuns which are called *minne di vergine,* of the obvious fact that the breast of Saint Agatha is none other than Mount Etna, that great breast of the earth, and of the obvious relationship between her martyrdom and the volcano's eruptions and the earth's rebirth. We talked of the Greek character of the people of Catania, and of some of their modes of speech which may undoubtedly go back to the period of the Greek colonies. We talked of the Greek tradition, of the beauty of life as a work of art, even of robbery as a work of art, and some marvelous tricks were described whereby crime vanishes completely beneath a gratuitous mass of ornament. One of my friends told a story which had recently been brought to an end by a sentence in the law courts. An old peasant couple at Paternò had an only daughter, still unmarried and a little too fat, for whom they wanted to find a husband. One day there arrived at their house (this was just after the war) a smart-looking man and woman who said they had been sent by a lawyer in Catania whose name—out of discretion—they did not give, but whose photograph they showed: a very fine young man, and rich into the bargain. He had sent them to find out whether he might ask for the daughter's hand in marriage. Although rather suspicious, the peasants invited him to come: then they would see. The following week the handsome lawyer arrived, together with his two companions. The girl fell in love with him, the marriage was arranged, and meanwhile the three of them were guests in the *contadino's* house, where they spent a week of festivity and junketing. After dinner one day, in the garden, the woman fell down underneath a tree and lay senseless: her companions shouted that she must not be touched, that she was in a trance, and that if she were awakened she might die. The woman heaved herself about, groaning and prophesying: she said that below the ground, in the exact place where she had fallen, there was buried treasure, but that this treasure could not be removed unless a virgin, the daughter of the house, were first publicly deflowered, there, in that same spot, underneath the tree. The old peasant, his wife and his daughter consulted together, and so great was their desire for the treasure that they submitted willingly to the condition: after all, it would merely be a question of anticipating the approaching marriage. So the ceremony took place under the tree, amid general gaiety; then they immediately started digging and a box full of gold appeared. The lawyer suggested going to Catania to show the gold to a goldsmith; but the car broke down after a few yards, and the journey was put off. But the lawyer and his companions had to leave, and, in the enthusiasm of the peasant and his family, managed, by some pretext or other, to get him to give them all his savings—seven hundred thousand lire; and off they went. Next day the peasant went joyfully to Catania with the box. The goldsmith, at the first glance, saw that the gold was nothing but the false money used at the *festa* of Saint Agatha. It had been bought, for twenty-one thousand lire, by the "lawyer," who was really a barber's assistant.

Our evening ended at the puppet play at the Teatro Garibaldi, where that remarkable man, Commendatore Insanguine, reproduces the stories of the paladins with his marionettes. They are extremely fine marionettes, almost as large as human beings, with beautiful faces, carved armor, clothes and weapons which Commendatore Insanguine has made entirely himself. They weigh from sixty to eighty pounds each; they are supported from above and are moved by two assistants, two young men who work in the citrus plantations by day and, in the evenings, at the puppet theater, for three hundred lire. They are marvelously skillful at moving them, even in the passages of arms and duels with violent gestures which take place to a rhythmical accompaniment of stamping feet imitating the roll of drums in a battle. I tried, after the performance, to hold and manipulate one of these paladins: it is heavy work. That evening they were giving one of the episodes of *Erminio della Stella d'Oro,* which runs, as a romance in instalments, for seventy-five evenings. The public knows beforehand what is going to happen and participates passionately. In this story Rinaldo and Roland and the other more famous paladins do not occur, but characters whom, I confess, I did not know, and who seemed to me, to tell the truth, slightly spurious. There were—I think I am right in saying—Aronte of Morocco, father of Erminio of the golden star, husband of Gemma della Fiamma (who in turn was daughter of Baisette of Persia); they were the parents of Tigreleone, protagonist of this adventure, which takes place at Berlin while it is being attacked by the Saracens and by Arnoldo, emperor of Russia. We saw terrible battles in which the Syrian hero Ideo killed the famous Tangisteo of Holland; was greeted by the daughter of the emperor of Russia with a cry of: "Ideuccio mio!"; and carried on a slaughter of his enemies until Arturo di Macera, an Italian wearing a big, ugly hat, came upon the scene, and shouting: "For me, an Italian, death is always glorious," hurled himself into the fray—which, however, would not come to an end until one of the following evenings. I took rather a dislike to the protagonist, Tigreleone, who was besieged not merely by Saracens and by Ideo but also by female warriors who were rivals and extremely jealous. I said to my neighbors that I should like to see him killed by the gallant Ideo, but they replied that if anything of that kind happened the theater

110

would be transformed into "The Valley" (meaning the Valley of Roncesvalles), full of corpses. The paladins are real and actual idols, far more so than Coppi or Bartali; people rejoice at their victories and weep when they die. I was told of a cabman who woke up one morning in a mood of black depression and told his family he would not be taking his cab out on to the square that day because it was a day of mourning: in the evening, at the Garibaldi Theater, Rinaldo would die.

Early next morning we left to make an excursion right around Mount Etna. It was a clear, calm day. The friends who were going with me wanted to take me, before we left the town, to the Bellini garden, where along the avenues are busts of the celebrated men of Catania, and where, also, is the labyrinth near which workmen are digging a deep ditch into which is to be put a young elephant that is shortly to arrive from Rome, and where they have taken the fragments of an excavated Vaccarini fountain. From there you can see a big lawn with an elephant, *U'liotro,** cut in grass, a *trinacria†*, an inscription, a star, enclosures for bands, some very green trees, some thickets of shrubs, and, beyond, the white and blue triangle of Etna against the sky. What an enchanting place for a background to childish memories! I wish I had been a native of Catania, to have run about these avenues as a little boy!

Coming out of Catania, the road at once crosses the

* The elephant is the crest of Catania.
† The symbol of Sicily; a woman's head with three legs.

sciara of Curia. It is a wonderful and terrible land-scape, black and purple and gray, of bare or lichen-covered lava blown by some prehistoric wind into strange, wrinkled waves. In the midst of the lava there is a new working-class quarter of white houses, like a city in the desert. We drove right across the *sciara* through different kinds of lava, some of it still unchanged after centuries, some of it crumbled and transformed: it is the plants which slowly make the stone into fertile soil. First come the fungi and mosses and lichens, red, green or gray, encrusting the purple basalt and breaking it up to the point where cardamom and then broom can take root, and another kind of broom called, in dialect, *cichiciaca.* Not until after the broom does the prickly pear make its appearance—plant of resurrection, the tree of the lava, tenderly green on the stony slopes. After the prickly pear come the other plants—the fig tree, the pistachio tree, the almond, the olive, and, lastly, the vine. Thus the stone which has flowed from the volcano can be dated from the plants which grow upon it, until the moment when another flow sub-merges the last vines and the olives and the prickly pears and the broom bushes and the lichens, and the stone desert comes back again.

Leaving the *sciara* behind, the road brought us to Misterbianco, into the midst of the ducal estates and memories of De Felice and the peasant risings. Further on another *sciara,* that of the year 1760, comes down from the Monti Rossi, the outposts of Etna. Through the most spendid orange groves we reached Paternò. Beyond the Simeto River appeared the mountain country of Centuripe, the naked interior of Sicily. The town had a festive look, and was full of garlands and lamps; preparations were going on for the feast of Saint Barbara during the next few days. We crossed the Via Fallica; but my companions assured me this was merely the name of a person. There was a crowd of people in front of the church: they were getting ready the car of Saint Barbara, sister saint of Saint Agatha, and the *cannelori,* the great wax candles, carved and engraved and painted, which were to be carried by hand in the procession. We went into the storehouse where the candles are kept, and the peasants who were there showed them to me. There was a candle for the carters and carriers, a candle for the laborers, a candle for the farmers, a candle for the bakers, a candle for the shopkeepers with great big pink angels on it ("This," the peasants told me, "is the drunkards' candle."). They were very proud of their own candle, the peasants' candle. All around it there were carved scenes of the saint's martyrdom. First of all, the tearing off of her breasts (for Saint Barbara, too —in the same way as, and perhaps even more than, Saint Agatha—is an Earth saint, a Mount Etna saint, sacred to fire and volcanic eruptions); then, Saint Barbara carried naked to her "shame," Saint Barbara in front of Christ, and, finally, her father, the Saracen king, cutting off her head.

Through herds of long-horned goats and extremely elegant cemeteries we went on to Santa Maria di

Licodia. "This is a quiet place," said the *contadino* who was one of my traveling companions. "Here Communists, Christian Democrats and Fascists all play cards together." Here, in far-off days, when Santa Maria di Licodia was called Etna Inessa, stood the famous temple of Vulcan or possibly of the more ancient local god of fire, Adrano, surrounded by a sacred wood which was guarded by a thousand dogs which were able, by divine instinct, to distinguish the good from the wicked. Farther on, on the mountainside, like a gray military fortress, stands the feudal castle of Baron Spitalieri. Beyond Biancavilla and its cemetery we arrived at Adrano, formerly Aderno, sacred, as its name implies, to lava and the gods of fire. In front of the Saracen castle opens out the valley of the Simeto, which every year has tremendous floods; and opposite, like a desolate and fantastic theatrical scene, are the mountains of Enna, with towns and villages perched on top of their bare summits—Centuripe, Regalbuto, Troina, and the feudal estates of Baron Spitalieri, Baron Solima and others. The Simeto is in truth a boundary line. On the near side Etna, visible high against the sky like some unattainable god, and Etna's realm, snowy wastes and basalt above, and then, as you come down, thickets of chestnut and bracken, and, lower still, vineyards and gardens and citrus groves and villages and green plantations, on a soil which is always crumbling and fortuitous but full of salts and abun-

114

dantly fertile, life-giving juices. On the far side, beyond the Simeto, lie desolate, bare feudal estates, corn country, but destitute, yellow, treeless, uninhabited, sun-smitten, mysterious in its nakedness, a far, remote world where the shining gods of the volcano have never set foot. We stopped only for a moment at Adrano, an illustrious town, full of history, rich in brigand enterprise (the brigands were once in league with the feudal lord but more recently have become isolated and independent), a center, both in former and in recent times, of working-class struggle, where only last year the laborer Girolamo Rosano was killed in a demonstration in the piazza. Farther on, far away on the mountains, Enna and Calascibetta appeared, and on the other side Cesarò and the bare mountains of the province of Messina. After another *sciara*, the Sciara Nova, one of the hundred that flow down like streams from Etna, we came into Bronte.

It was now midday, and here we stopped, partly because of the hour, partly because my companions had friends here, partly for the charm of the name— from Brontes the Cyclops who, with his companions Steropes and Arges made, according to Hesiod, Jove's thunderbolts. It is a large village without any beauty of architecture but with good houses along its main street. It, too, is rich in history, like Adrano, and like Randazzo to which it was once subject. It is known especially for its former connection with the duchy of the same name, Nelson's feudal estate.

Bronte is also known for its continual peasant risings and revolts, and for the ferocious acts of repression by Nino Bixio. While we were looking round for some trace of these historic memories, some peasants recognized me and invited me to visit their homes. So we left the main street and the richer quarter and went down, by steep, narrow lanes, into the *cortili*, or courts, inhabited by the poor. Rarely can such abject poverty be seen in this luxuriant countryside, at the foot of this most famous and fertile volcano, in this climate that is inhabited by the most famous of the gods. We visited several of these *cortili* (a *cortile*, here, is a sort of small widening in the road, round which are built huts): men, and women beckoned to us from doorways to come in and see the conditions in which they lived. For lack of drainage, streams of foul water flow along the ground, through the streets and the sloping *cortili*, and the smell catches you in the throat. The houses —if they can be so called—are mere hovels with roofs of reeds through which the rain comes; they are smoky and bare and windowless, and eight, or ten, or twelve people live huddled together in a few square yards. The children, with faces lovely as angels', have stomachs swollen with malaria: it is a spectacle of the utmost peasant misery, unexpected in this paradisal stretch of country. In the Cortile dei Garofani—Carnation Court—where the stink of sewerage is unbearable, where you don't know where to put your foot amongst the trickling black water, we went into the hut of a tenant farmer, or *mezzadro,* of a hectare and a half of land.* There were eight of them in the half-roofless house; the two youngest children, Angelo and Nunziata, looked at me with the large eyes that are typical of malarial children. The father, who is the owner of his own hut, told me that he had to pay rates of fifteen hundred lire a year on it to the town council—the rate for *nettezza urbana* or town cleaning. The same sights were to be seen everywhere: in the Cortile delle Magnolie, in the Piazza della Fortuna, in the Via Lorenzo il Magnifico, in the Via Pietro Aretino, in the Via delle Muse—strange names bestowed by the poetical taste of some alderman of the town upon these foul sewers. I asked the peasants of the Via delle Muse if they knew who these amiable goddesses were.

"We don't know," they answered; "we're just ignorant people—how should we know? But perhaps," said one of them, who had a wide-awake, intelligent face, "perhaps it can be interpreted as some sort of a nickname." (*Ingiuria,* the Sicilian word for a nickname, means also an insult.) These names are truly an insult.

In the Cortile delle Magnolie the women complained. "We have a special kind of democracy in

* A *mezzadro* is a tenant on the crop-sharing, or *métayage,* system; 1½ hectares is about 3.7 acres.

this town," they said. "The bosses stay in the piazza, and anyone else can die, if they want to."

In one house, which was hardly more than three yards square, lived ten Christians.

"How do you sleep?"

"At night," they explained, "we lie like sardines in a tin."

There was a water tap, however, in one corner; but a new, shining meter, which seemed larger than the house, was stuck on the tap.

"When it rains," said one of the men, "we have to put on our Napoleon boots."

In the Via Pindaro there was a woman who knew the person after whom the street was called. "Pindar," she said to me, "was a Bronte man, a barber who lived here."

There is one laborer who has a house which can only be entered on all fours, and it costs him five hundred lire a month in rent. In the Cortile delle Orchidee there are foul streams of water. A young wife looked at me with a desolate air and said, in a very gentle voice: "What we need is proper lavatories, with proper drains."

That is how the laboring class lives in Bronte— thousands of landless peasants who are waiting for land under the land reform scheme; who for a century and a half have been fighting a daily peasant war against a persisting feudal system for the lands of the duchy, which from time to time they rise to occupy as they did in 1848 and in the period just after the last war; who are turned out and then go back patiently, tenaciously, and who remain in spite of everything, full of human vitality, and still manage, in their fetid courtyards, to have hope in the future.

The center of their thoughts, that which they consider the origin of their miseries, the land of their hopes, is the duchy: so we made up our minds to go and visit it. We went down to the bridge, which crosses the river Simeto at a point where it cuts deeply through the rock, in a fault in the earth's crust. From here, the view of Bronte on its hill and, behind it, the new outline of Etna seen from the northwest, rising impassively with its smokeholes clear against the sky, contrast marvelously with the barren slopes of the feudal lands at our backs. We could go no further because the road was blocked, so we took the other road, toward Randazzo and Passo Pisciaro. On the road we encountered inhabitants of Tortorici, tall, big men, and then, passing through flows of lava both old and recent, came back into the desert, over which hangs Etna, lonely and bare; and then the flat plain of the duchy appears, in which rise the three affluents of the Simeto—the Martello, the Cuto and the Saraceno—and beyond it desolate mountains over which cloud-shadows were passing. On the slopes of the mountains could be seen, very small, the straw stacks—or rather, the little cone-shaped structures made of straw—with small, low doors, in which the peasants of the mountains live, all higgledy-piggledy. We went quickly down to the Castello di Maniaci, the castle of Admiral Lord Nelson and his heirs. There is a very ancient church there, with a Byzantine Madonna, a courtyard between stone walls which have something of the barracks and the prison about them, and, in the middle, a lava cross with the inscription:

HEROI

IMMORTALI

NILI

Here are the offices of the duchy, a post office, and the police. The actual owner is not here at present. The history of Maniaci would need a whole book to tell it fully. To put it briefly, this land, won by the Byzantine warrior Giorgio Maniace in 1040 from the Saracens, given to Giovanni Calafato in 1221 by Frederick II, given to Giovanni Ventimiglia by King Martin in 1396, passing later to the Ospedale Grande e Nuovo of Palermo, and finally presented to Horatio Nelson by King Ferdinand of Bourbon in 1799 as a reward for having saved the kingdom by getting rid of the liberals of Naples—this land has changed masters, but its peasants have continued to live in the same straw stacks, unchangingly, for a thousand years. But the struggle for the land is fiercer than ever: one of the many anachronistic examples of the survival of a vanished world of feudalism, of its transformations, and of the stubborn attempts of the peasants to exist as human beings. This long and complicated affair really deserves to be recounted in full: how this estate was confiscated during the war as being foreign property, and how English officers rushed to take possession of it again on the day of liberation, how it has now been declared subject to expropriation under the plans of the Sicilian land reform, how the administration, naturally enough, is making every possible effort to oppose land reform, even by anticipating in its own way, as has happened in other cases, and how the peasants are reacting to the duchy's moves. The last episodes in this protracted war are so complex, an almost inextricable tangle of legal acts, law suits, decrees, restrictions, interacting and conflicting interests, that it would be impossible to give the whole story here —nor could I myself have imagined it, if I had not had firsthand evidence.

We were going around the fields talking to the peasants who were crowding about us, moved by their endless need to protest, when one of them stated with passion, violence, and sorrow that to avoid expropriation the duchy had forced them to buy the land on which they worked by the threat that the land would be sold to others and they themselves driven out immediately from their work: and these forced sales took place, to a large extent, after the final date agreed to by the Sicilian reform law, December 27, 1950. "Those of us peasants who didn't have the money, we were told to borrow it. With the moneylenders of Tortorici and Randazzo, interest is at 35, 40, or even 50 per cent. We paid a high price for the land. We had to sell our cows and our belongings to pay the first installment, so as not to be turned out of our houses. The land has to be paid for within five years: God only knows how we will manage with our debts. If we can't pay an installment, we lose the land." Thus, according to this man, the peasants, forced to acquire the land, find themselves in debt, ruined, and owners of land sold after the legal date limit and therefore liable to be expropriated by the land reform and given to others; and consequently at war among themselves as well as with the landless laborers of Bronte. They had to pay the expenses of the deed of acquisition, whereas Horatio Nelson, on the contrary, when he received Bronte as a gift, was exempted by the generous Bourbon from playing the sum due for the titles of investiture. While the peasants were telling me about these matters, some armed *campieri* (field guards) went past and looked at us with suspicion. There is a feeling of feudal terror in the very atmosphere. I looked around and saw in the distance, coming up the path, a square-shouldered man, dressed in a light suit, with his hat pushed back. As he walked up, he looked me over with his very black eyes set in a round, pallid face. He was an official of the duchy. From my clothes he could see I was a stranger, a gentleman, and from the peasants' faces and gestures he could imagine what had been said. He stopped, greeted me, and whispered, "Don't pay attention to what the peasants say. They always complain, but it's all propaganda, nothing but propaganda. The land, the duchy offered it, of its own accord, before the reform, massed with the lands requisitioned by the prefect of Catania, for the good of the peasants—almost five thousand acres for long term lease or out-right ownership. It isn't the duchy's fault if the actual sale took place after the legal time limit: they made us wait so that the distribution would take place during elections. The duke wanted to start a model farm which would have been to everyone's advantage, but he met with all sorts of difficulties—the water supply was expropriated as long as thirty years ago—and opposition from all sides, from the peasants and from the land reform authorities, from the regional government and from the state. We had started with the school, the mill, the infirmary, the pharmacy. We have always helped the peasants, but they are not grateful. At one time they used to kiss our hands, but now resentment has been stirred up. Without us, they couldn't exist. For instance, we have set up a syndicate: by themselves, they couldn't manage. Come to the office, I'll show you the documents, our reclamation plans. Don't listen to them." And he walked away.

A skinny little peasant arrived on horseback. He was one of those, so he proclaimed immediately from high up on his horse, who had been compelled to buy the land, and he was in despair. "We're just outcast dogs," he said to me, "as we were in the time of the Saracens." His face set in pain and anger, he told how he had had to sell his cows, borrow money from a usurer at Tortorici, pay forty thousand lire for the deed; and he did not know how he was going to manage to live. Another one came up, and a third and a fourth; and each one expounded to me, giving me precise figures, his accounts, his expenses, his profits, his debts, all of them convinced that they were pawns in a complex and insidious plan to save the landowners from the land reform, while at the same time crushing the force of the peasants' resistance by dividing them up, pitting the new peasant owners against the land-hungry laborers, discouraging both and confining them in endless bondage. They feel wretched and abandoned, surrounded by hostile powers and maneuverings, confined in their own ancient and impervious diffidence and in the desolate patience of fatigue: but now, they say, they will know how to protect themselves. "Here in the flat country," they said to me, "it's not so bad. But go up onto the mountain, take a look at the people in the straw huts, who live like animals; lots of those who were born up there, their births haven't even been reported to the civil authorities—nobody knows how many of them there are."

We left the duchy considerably troubled. Is it fated, perhaps, that things should remain forever in the same state of crystallized ferocity and that the peasant must always struggle, unarmed, against feudal lords, heroes of the sea, administrative lawyers? Here, as everywhere in peasant districts, there are from time to time bloody insurrections, revolts which end in death. Here at Bronte, from the 2nd to the 5th of August, 1860, there was a popular uprising for the division of the land, the peasants being urged on by Garibaldi's promises and by their usual ancient hope. Naturally, as always happens in these peasant outbreaks, it was a fierce revolt, and there were many dead among the Bourbonite gentry, and many houses burned down. In the eyes of the peasants of Bronte the victory of Garibaldi could have only one meaning—possession of the land and freedom from feudalism; and in the name of Garibaldi they started to massacre the landowners. They were ahead of their times. Garibaldi, under pressure from the British consul at Catania, who was afraid for the fate of the duchy, sent Nino Bixio to restore order. Nino Bixio arrived when things were already quiet, another of Garibaldi's men, Colonel Poulet, having already entered Bronte in a peaceful manner with a company of soldiers. Bixio was ferocious. After a mere show of a trial he immediately shot the leaders of the revolt, among whom was a lawyer, Nicolo Lombardo, a liberal who had previously led the Bronte uprisings of '48.

The first shades of evening were slanting down from Etna, and bright spindles of cloud, drawn out by the wind, stretched horizontally round the crater. We came into Randazzo by the ancient gate between the castle and the church of dark lava and white stone. It is a historic town, but we went hurriedly past its black convents, its black churches, its black houses, through its black streets, hastening toward the vineyards of Linguaglossa. The moon, full and round, had now risen high in the heavens, illuminating lava flows and thickets with a cold light. Already, far away beyond Fiumefreddo, we could see the gleaming sea, and over this gleaming sea, in the far distance, the mountain above Taormina had an unearthly look. The painted fishing boats were putting out from the shore, the lights of their lanterns shining on the green water like twinkling constellations.

2

As soon as we got out of the car, in the piazza at Aci Trezza, with the first drops of rain falling we stopped to look at the façade of the Church of San Giovanni. It looked, in real life, smaller than it appears to be in *La terra trema*, and against the damp gray-blue of the sky its whiteness seemed different from the unforgettable, tender, livid whiteness of dawn with which it came into view at the beginning of Visconti's film. Behind us were the black reefs of the Cyclops, and the sea, which was becoming smooth and gray and seemed to be flattening itself out at the approach of the shower, like a cat waiting to be stroked. Already the rain, carried by a light, gusty wind, was coming down harder: so we ran hastily up the steps and took refuge inside the little restaurant. We thought, as we went in, of La Santuzza with her "Daughter of Mary" medal, of old Uncle Santoro, the blind man sitting with his stick in the doorway, of poor 'Ntoni Malavoglia turned out of the inn like

127

a mangy dog. We thought of Verga, and inside the room it was all Visconti. I thought I recognized the girls whom we asked for something to eat and who brought us fish fresh from the sea and shellfish and sea urchins: and indeed it was they, with their very gentle, charming faces and their ways that were filled with a transient yet eternal grace who had taken the leading parts in *La terra trema*. The elder one was with child: she had been married since the film and was expecting her first baby: the change in her face and body had not taken away her look of almost animal reserve, but had merely lent to her gracefulness an added solemnity. The times of the film were a long way off now, as also the dreams and the strange hopes that had been born of it; life had returned to its usual course, and the household was about to be enlarged by the addition of a new baby.

By the time we had finished our sea urchins, our *occhi di bue* and other delicious shellfish, the rain had stopped and a pinkish sun was filtering through the sea haze. We hurried out and went down to the sea. After going down a flight of steps, we passed near a fountain in the course of excavation by workmen; but I do not know if it was being removed or merely taken to another position. A painter who had come from Catania had set up his easel and was busy finishing a brightly-colored picture of boats. The boats were drawn up on the beach among the great polished, purple stones very close together, so that it was difficult to walk between them. We looked down from above upon this expanse of stones and boats, and on the sea which was blue and green again in the sunshine, and the strange lumps of rock that the Cyclops had hurled from Mount Etna at the fleeing Ulysses, and the fishermen mending their nets on slabs of rock on the beach, and the boys playing among the boats, and an old man with a brush touching up the varnish of his painted boat, and some tar smoke in the distance, and at the corner of the street a fisherman selling the fish he had just caught—a world full of light, quiet, enclosed in its own harmonious movements. On the house to the left the modern bas-relief dedicated to the Malavoglias stood out conspicuously, and beneath it, in abbreviated form, was inscribed Verga's phrase: ". . . and these poor creatures left abandoned on the lava flow, at that hour, were like souls in Purgatory." We thought of the girls at the restaurant, who, in Visconti's film, as they stood on the *sciara,* with the sea behind, their great black shawls flapping in the wind, had become, not so much souls in Purgatory, as astonishing, frightened birds from Hell.

Everything here, then, called up some image or other—the *Odyssey, I Malavoglia, La terra trema;* and we wondered what was the precise enchantment of this village which is now so intimately connected with the art to which it has given birth. As we walked past the fisherman, who was holding a small swordfish in his hand and whose face had in it something of the fish's sharp, silvery quality, I heard my name called and turned around. It was a young foreign lady whom I knew and who was making a voyage of discovery round Sicily. "Have you noticed?" she said. "This is the most beautiful village in the world." Her enthusiasm was quite natural and direct. She knew nothing of classical mythology, nor had she ever even heard of Verga or Visconti. I asked her why she admired Aci Trezza more than all the other villages. Nature, here, was pleasing to her, she said —the color of the air, of the sea, of the earth, the black of the lava, the purple of the basalt, the primeval disorder of the seashore, Etna high in the heavens, the modest, civilized, pink houses; but more than anything it was the human inhabitants that moved her, their attitude toward life and death. She had come from Taormina, she told me, in a hired car; and the driver, at the first expanses of lava, had begun telling her, with a kind of strange, enthusiastic, admiring nostalgia, of the eruptions of Etna that he had seen. She, thinking of the fields and houses destroyed, and of the dead, had asked him: "Weren't you afraid of being killed?"

"But that is life," the chauffeur had answered.

Afterward, as she went round the streets of Aci Trezza, it had seemed to her, said this foreign lady, that she was moving among a population of gods, so clear was it in each one of them that his face, his gestures, his vicissitudes, his destiny were, so to speak, eternal and eternally fixed, in pursuance, not of a spontaneous, capricious individual story, but of a style or a custom which was common to all and immutable, shining only in each one of them with a different grace.

"They don't seem to me to be men and women and children of today, but trees in a forest, or antique beings like the gods. Their looks and their gestures are like those of statues: the fishermen, both young and old, have necks like statues. It seems to me that everything here must always have been thus and always will be thus. Then I understood what the chauffeur meant; death is always present, with that volcano and with the sea, but it is as though it did not exist, because the fate of those who remain alive will be the same as that of the dead: they will have the same gestures, the same way of accepting things, the same way of wrapping themselves in their shawls and walking with the grace of animals or of princes. That is why this little village seems to me eternal and wonderfully beautiful."

We had gone down, meanwhile, onto the shore, among the boats: they were like brightly-colored flowers, like the Sicilian carts without their wheels, with saints painted on them and inscriptions round their edges. Almost all of them had two saints—San Francesco da Paola, patron saint of sailors (like the Malavoglias' boat *Provvidenza,* "with the lovely red stripe along the edge and, on the stern, Saint Francis with a beard that looked as though it were made of cotton wool"), and also the San Giovanni of the church at Aci Trezza. Some of them have curious inscriptions on them: "I am beautiful because I perform my own tasks." Many of them, with the elongated line of their bows, look like fish, like big swordfish, and, to increase the resemblance, have an open eye—which forms the eye of the fish—painted on the prow, like that on the cheek of the fisherman of Cnossos. Upon one old, repainted boat (was this, perhaps, the *Provvidenza* of 'Ntoni Malavoglia?) was written:

IL COMANTO LO DO IO
LA PROVIDENZA LA DÀ DIO

A bright sun was shining, now, in a sky that had cleared: sitting on the edge of a boat we looked at the sea. In that transparent, clean light things assumed an open, shining countenance, and the nocturnal shadow of the Malavoglias seemed to dissolve and vanish away. It is a nocturnal book, I reflected as I warmed myself in the sunshine; everything in it happens in the evening, in the darkness of narrow lanes, in the blackness of the *sciara,* during a storm, during the night; the sea is scarcely ever anything but black, black like the lava, or the color of lead. Spring, and greenness, and sunshine make their appearance only for fleeting moments and as if lost in the shadow of night; the only light, sometimes, is the moon—"weeping under the medlar-tree in the moonlight." The only noise, apart from the sound of words, is the noise of carts at night. The faces of people, the look of the landscape, are never described. It might be thought that Verga, in order to enter into the destinies of his characters, had first had to

132

renounce all mention of their faces and their general appearance, of the sea and the countryside, and of beauty: "and now that it was impossible to see either the sea or the country, it looked as if there were nothing else in the world but Trezza."

Verga's vision was confined to his own world; it identified itself with that of the fisherman, of the gossip, of the grandfather or the daughter, and with their commonplace, patient, obscure destinies. Therefore, until the dawn on the last page, both sea and countryside and individualized appearances of human beings must disappear. In Visconti the opposite occurs, for he participates in things and understands them without identifying himself with them, and is therefore all eyes, vision and imagery. He is the modern epic in contrast to the romance of Verga. And Verga's romance is an impossible thing and therefore all the more singular, since it is of a world which is, in its very essence, antagonistic to romance, a world of epic antiquity.

As we left, the girls at the restaurant—those modest heroines—bowed to us, with wayward grace, from the doorway.

THREE

THREE

1

Summer strikes down Sicily like a yellow hawk on the yellow, stubble-covered expanses of the feudal lands. The light multiplies itself in, as it were, a continuous explosion, and seems to open up and reveal the fantastic shapes of the mountains and to make sky, earth and sea compact and hard as steel, in a single, uninterrupted wall of bright-colored metal. Beneath the infinite weight of this light, men and animals move in silence, actors, perhaps, in some remote drama of which the words do not reach our ears: but their gestures hang in the luminous air like mutable, petrified voices, like trunks of the prickly pear, twisted fronds of olive, monstrous rocks, bottomless black caves.

We, too, came down out of the sky, like the hawk of summer. After an hour's flight, sailing through a liquid land of gray cloud, of sudden, tender patches of sky blue or gleaming sea gray, among rivers, mists and distillations of wetness, enclosed in an airy universe of water, all at once—as though some hand, with an unexpected gesture, had thrust aside the vapors and laid bare the horizons to the light—we could see below us, tragic, vivid, improbable, the blue of Sicily, and the coast, and the burnt skeleton of Monte Pellegrino. As though sucked down by this magnetic, voracious land, we found ourselves, even before we had had time to contemplate it, on the landing strip of the airport at Bocca di Falco.

Behind the low wooden barrier a crowd was awaiting the passengers, a real black, agitated crowd, moved by some unexplained universal excitement or passion. I saw them there, impatient for someone's arrival: there were at least forty people, men, women and children, a little band of peasants in their best clothes, the men in black and the old women with veils on their heads, the girls in light, bright-colored cotton dresses, the little girls with their ribbons in their hair; they were all pointing toward the airplane and crying: "There she is! There she is! There she is!" They were all standing, crowded and crammed together, at the barrier, waiting. Who could it be that was arriving, so eagerly expected? Somebody told me they had been for hours at the airport, having come in a group all from the same village, and that for hours they had been looking at the sky and listening for the sound of an engine, and repeating, at every false alarm: "There she is! There she is!" And now, at last, she appeared; she was the last to come out of the plane.

She was a woman of middle age, tall and bulky,

red in the face, her heavy, peasant-housewife figure garbed in good-quality American clothes. She had a big leather bag on her arm, high-heeled shoes and silk stockings—the only silk stockings among the cotton stockings of all the women who were waiting for her and who, in one moment, surrounded her. Behind her, to one side, walked a much more elderly man, wearing a Panama hat, a showy tie, and a bright pink, flowered shirt—obviously her husband, an emigrant of long ago, coming back home with his wife. But it was she who was so eagerly awaited, it was she round whom the crowd closed with a passionate pressure that could find no words. Then the greetings and embraces and recognitions began. First of all her mother—a little old woman dressed in black, with a beautiful peasant face, antique and noble, reaching scarcely up to the shoulder of this big daughter of hers, who was made even taller by her hat, and who was embarrassed by the forgotten gestures that suddenly came back to her; for she had walked across to the barrier with the steps of a town dweller and now encountered, like a memory of childhood, a different way of moving, her mother's way. The two women, encircled by the crowd, embraced with tears, crying out and moaning with a joy that seemed like the deepest sorrow; then they separated for a moment, only to embrace again with further wailing, beating each other on the back, rocking and swaying as though pushed by some external force, by some wind of passion, and touching and feeling each other as though to make sure of each other's physical presence, and then beginning their endless embracings and groanings all over again. This greeting of mother and daughter had the same piercing intensity as a funeral lament—so much so that I and the other travelers who were brought to a halt by the spectacle of it felt rising within us, not merely a smile, but a kind of painful lump in the throat, and tears came involuntarily into our eyes. Then still held, still touched by her mother, whose hands and eyes never left her, she began her greetings, in hierarchical order, to the rest of her relations, and her acknowledgments, in succession, of each one of the others. Brothers and sisters, perhaps, whose image had been blurred by time, and brothers-in-law and sisters-in-law whom she had never met before, and cousins, godfathers, and remoter kindred, and the children of all these, born after her departure and now thrust forward, one by one, into her embrace; some of these already big, others so small as to arouse a glow of gratified tenderness in the midst of all the tears. But by this time the agonizing ceremony of the maternal embraces was starting all over again.

The "American" woman was returning, after goodness knows how long, to her native land. A Negro leaning languidly against the doorpost, in a blue uniform, a camera hung round his neck and a little thin mustache on his fleshy upper lip, looked on with a detached and superior air at this scene which to him, apparently, seemed barbarous. Half an hour, perhaps, passed in this way before I made up my mind to leave the airport. (The woman who had been welcomed with such heartrending passion had emigrated at a very early age and had been away from Sicily for almost thirty years. She had raked up from her savings the necessary three thousand dollars for the journey, so as to go back to see her mother and her native village again; and the three thousand dollars had been stolen from her as she came out of the bank. Opinion in America had been stirred by this event, and a public subscription had made it possible for her to come back and rediscover those forgotten gestures at the Bocca di Falco airport.)

After that we drove among crowds of children through the streets of the far-reaching suburbs and came into wonderful Palermo through the Norman gate. Here was the yellow cathedral and the tombs of the Swabian kings, and the enchanted palm gardens. In a corner of the garden there was a dense group of people in a circle, listening intently to the words of a man who was sitting on a little low chair telling a story. In his hand he held a white walking stick, which he tapped rhythmically on the ground according to the movement of his story: he talked with his eyes closed, his face was very pale, his mouth mournful, his clothes poor and patched. He appeared to be blind, a blind bard: and he was, indeed, a professional storyteller. He was telling the story of Roger of Sicily, the endless tale of his loves, of the despair of the beautiful lady who thought she was betrayed and deserted, and of how Roger snatched her away and set her free, of how they were surrounded in the enemy city, and of how they succeeded in passing through the gates—a long and endless narrative; and the people, sitting all round him, listened to him in silence, working-class people, old men, children, never losing a syllable or a gesture or a detail of the prose and the tapping stick and the sad, solemn play of facial expression, all in the monotonous convention of an archaic, epic idiom. But now, all unaware, the enemy warriors reach the gates, arms clash, the battle begins, with flashing of swords: and prose, little by little, turns into poetry, and the telling of the tale changes in rhythm and quantity, and the words are broken up according to cadence and accent, like the metrical chant of an ancient poem. It is another language, the rhythmic language of arms, growing ever more agitated and rapid and spasmodic, with a prosody of cut and thrust, of skirmish and parry and feint, of wounds and death, like a sacred warrior dance; an astounding evocation of times long past. Swifter and swifter, more and more resplendent came the flow of words—broken at the fall of the accent, the longs and shorts more and more heavily stressed; until at last Roger was left victorious and alone; and the bard fell silent, and opened his eyes that were soft as black velvet.

2

Velvety black eyes followed me everywhere in the streets of Palermo. The first had been those of the storyteller, which had opened only at the end of his rhythmic chant, when he had risen and gone round with his saucer, divesting himself of his "blind poet of antiquity" appearance. But how many other eyes there were, everywhere, eyes of men and of women, black with a blackness that was both velvety and shining, lacking the dark shadow of the tears of countless vigils which gives a look of earthy nobility to the eyes of the peasants of Lucania, but instead, full of fire, of a black, sparkling fire, tender and at the same time fierce, languid and mild and dramatic, full, not so much of expression and feeling, as of vitality, of entreaty, of a moist, animal fixity, soft, impenetrable, throbbing like the star of Venus in a black sky! The glances that issue forth from these furnaces of hell or paradise meet and cross each other from all directions in the swarming streets

143

with a mute violence that weighs heavy, that imposes itself upon you, so that in a short time all you can see is these thousands and thousands of eyes, with their demanding, inviting, savagely wayward look and their alternate display and concealment of a vehement beauty lit up and then hidden by a glance of the same black profundity as the velvety curtain of the night sky that so jealously covers the illuminated city.

There was something unaccustomed, something festive in the air that day, which made the glances of the girls softer than usual: it was an important evening, when they could go out wearing their new dresses and stay out until late at night. The workmen had now finished hanging up yellow and pink lamps—oranges and lemons of fire—on the trees, and festoons and arches of lamps along the streets and on the palaces; and with nightfall, all of a sudden, the whole town caught fire. The big street that goes right across Palermo, the Via Maqueda, and the Via Ruggero Settimo, shone like an endless arcade of lights, the Viale della Libertà was like a sparkling orange grove: seen from a distance, from the narrow streets that are a continuation of it, it looked like a great rising expanse of ground covered with an innumerable crowd of people, or like a mountain meadow, or an immense slanting wall mounting up until it touched the sky. The side streets were brilliant too; the Quattro Canti, with their statues and moldings, were like the wings of a sumptuous seventeenth century theater. A whole people, with its countless eyes, was moving silently round in that bath of light, coming out from the palaces of princes and barons and from the lanes and byways, and mingling together in the streets. The three round domes of the mosque, in the shadow of the Romanesque *campanile*, the baroque church and the neo-classical Bellini Theater, stood out red against the sky. In the Piazza Bologni, in front of the ruins of the ancient palace which was once the Fascist headquarters and is now a mere expanse of calcined walls behind a black façade, with white washing hung up and bits of white plaster which also look like white washing, the statue of Charles V, white in its marble armor— dedicated to Charles V, *Hassiaco/Saxonico/Germanico Hispanico Gallico/Africano Turcico/Mexicano Peruano Molucense/Imperatori Ter Maximo/*to the beggar king leaning on a stick—throws its shadow on the spectacular, crumbling façade of dilapidated imperial abodes. Here Garibaldi stopped (he appears to have stopped everywhere). There is the following inscription, on a large stone:

IN QUESTA ILLUSTRE CASA

IL 27 MAGGIO 1860

PER SOLE DUE ORE

POSÒ LE STANCHE MEMBRA

GIUSEPPE GARIBALDI

SINGOLARE PRODEZZA

FRA L'IMMANE SCOPPIO

DELLE MICIDIALI ARMI DA GUERRA

Tyranny, I fear, was able to take advantage of that
sleep. But this evening, with the noise of the fireworks, even that genius would not have gone to sleep.
It was the second evening of the *festa* which goes on
for three days in honor of the patron saint, the virgin Rosalia who freed Palermo from the plague. Her
colossal statue no longer stands on Monte Pellegrino; the two great heads struck off by lightning are
no longer there, nor yet the steep path up which
the faithful climbed. They are building a road and
awaiting the completion of a new monument by the
sculptor De Lisi, the author, if I am not mistaken, of
a statue at the main post office which is perfectly at-
tuned to its colossal pillars; and it is said that the
cardinal wishes to have a votive lighthouse erected
up there as well. Now that her true rocky abode is
deserted, the saint seems to have come down into
the town to envelop herself in the most luminous
possible form of love. The most irrational and un-
historic, too, seeing that not one of the many Paler-
mitans whom I have asked for the story of this highly
illustrious saint has been able to tell me of her adventures (possibly because these devotees of hers
whom I asked were all, like her, of immemorial

* Literal translation: In this illustrious house, on May 27th, 1860, for
two hours only, Giuseppe Garibaldi rested his weary limbs. With
singular bravery, amid the furious clash of deadly weapons of war,
he slept serenely, the genius who was the destroyer of all tyranny.

princely blood). In the streets, people were carrying her banner—little stiff banners of pink paper with borders and fringes like the rays of a sun and a blue picture in the center. Sellers of jasmine were going about on silent feet with their trophies of flowers stuck into reeds or straws to imitate a fragrant natural flowering, and the scent of them spread out in broad waves of sweetness. Other flowers were being sold everywhere, and salted pumpkin seeds, and roasted beans, and olives. In the unreal light two children came into view carrying monkeys on their backs. In the shop windows were Santa Rosalia ices, red and green, like a child's chalk drawings.

I turned into a lane, sloping down from the Via Maqueda, attracted by the gleaming wonder of fruit and fish stalls—precious piles of jewels beneath the balconies of the poor; and went on down through a labyrinth of streets and lanes and alleyways into an endless market where all the fruits of earth and sea seemed vivified with an impossible beauty, where the swordfish raised its weapon and its black fin toward the sky and the melons were blazing red under a roof of colored lamps like some hidden treasure from the Arabian Nights. This is the Vucceria. Whether its name comes from *boucherie,* as some philologists think, or, more simply, from *voce, voceria,* as others maintain, this swarming, excited place is a sapphire of the Orient that gleams with a theatrical vitality. I went down among the stalls, each one of which is an unexpected structure of flamelike forms, vegetable and animal, brilliantly colored, exaggerated, enormous, almost intolerable in size and intensity, its price cards painted red and yellow and the numbers on them drawn with indented edges in the same style as the carts. The lanes grew even narrower toward the sea, and I came out of the Vucceria into wretched little streets where children were lying stretched on the ground like untethered animals, and girls were coming out of doors half underground; all was movement and animation, everyone was on the way to the waterfront; and I too went there, for the great competition was about to begin, the *gioco dei fuochi,* the "Play of fire," of Santa Rosalia's Day. That is what fireworks are called here, and in truth there is nothing of "work" about them, and nothing artful or artificial; they are, so to speak, aerial games, free movements of the soul, a spontaneous and tumultuous expression, a resounding, dazzling portrait, of a country and a people. Everybody was going toward the sea, in groups and steadily growing parties, and I went with them, until, near the Palazzo Trabia, whither I had been directed, the crowd became an almost impenetrable wall. From here it extended, like a black, moving stretch of water, along the broad waterfront, as far as the eye could reach, right to the black background formed by the sea—a singularly silent crowd that seemed to be timidly awaiting a miracle. From the balcony of the Palazzo I now saw it swarming beneath me, thousands and thousands of indistinguishable people. And then, all of a sudden came the first, isolated explosion announcing the start of the

148

competition. There were three competitors, each of them with a great reputation, ancient masters of the craft of fireworks, who this evening would be contesting against one another like paladins in the tournament in honor of the saint. The silence of the crowd grew denser and the contest began. It was the most extraordinary firework display that one could possibly see: two hours of continuous din and coruscation.

The first of the paladins entered the field armed with a classic, harmonious art. Towers and bursts of flame, candles, multiple fireworks that gave repeated explosions going both up and down, Catherine wheels, colored representations of flowers, castles, waterfalls, fountains, the image of the saint surrounded with flowers of fire, and, at last, the grand final medley; it was all in perfect order and perfect proportion, both in time, in color and in light, recalling the traditional modulations of a perfect page of prose. It ended amid applause; and immediately the second competitor began. From his very first appearance, from the first launching of his thundering rockets into the sky, he took everyone's breath away with a savage assault of clamorous, dramatic violence. The rhythm of the explosions grew ever more compact, the glittering points of light more profuse, like an army of horses let loose in the charge or the overwhelming whirl of an avalanche. But in that violence—which seized you in the stomach and pushed you to an extreme of delicious anguish—you could feel the rhythm of the storyteller's heroic verses, the accent of the words in his epic song; and in the brilliant points of light you could see the flash of swords, and in the Catherine wheels and the castles and the pictures, the caparisons of the horses and the medieval cloaks and flowers on the bloody lawns of the tiltyard. Archaic, fierce, barbarous, gory, this play of fire went on, breathlessly, to its end, louder and louder, steadily increasing, endlessly multiplied, on and on, almost unendurable, to its grand final explosion; and then silence.

After such a marvel, what could the third paladin, who entered the field immediately afterward, possibly do? Still carried away by that epic poem of violence and colored rhythm, I scarcely looked at him. There was a slow return to the most exquisite refinement, the most delicate colors, to the white, sparkling cascade, like a cool refreshment in burning heat, to an ingenious, erudite originality of representation; and he, too, knew how to attain, very gradually, to a climax and then consummate it all of a sudden, at the moment of extreme intensity, and, after the climax, bring back the black, silent night.

The crowd was dispersing now through the narrow lanes toward the main streets, tired, happy, still absorbed and stupefied by that fire-induced sensuality, exhausted by that blinding orgasm. Tomorrow would come rest and refreshing sleep, and the long, slow procession, the return of the saint to her virgin bed, there, in the silent cathedral.

3

But the next day I was no longer there. I was not
recovering, with the crowd, from the exhaustion of
its collective orgasm, but had risen early and was
driving with some new friends eastward along the
road to Trapani and far-off Erice. The driver of the
car, that day, was unusual in that he was both a
chauffeur and one who had been elected by the people
to an important administrative position. He was a
dark, round-faced young man, full of good sense and
of the kind of culture which is both natural and
also acquired from experience and from enthusiasm
for active reality, and which, though far removed
from classical humanism, is nevertheless the more
live of the two. This enthusiasm, I realized at once,
showed itself also in the way he handled the car; it
was an Appia which had been fitted with a special
kind of silencer that made it roar like a hungry lion,
so that the noise it made sounded like that of a racing
car and made women turn round and passers-by

jump out of the way. And the quickened speed with which he hurled himself round bends in the road, the assertion of personality and at the same time the confidence in the future! I had, then, this unusual driver, and, when I thought of his responsibilities, I felt I was a sort of Don Quixote who

Doncellas curaban dél
Princesas de su rocino.

Alfio had been a workman in the naval dockyards, and had been dismissed some time before because he was a member of the workers' committee and he knew perfectly well that in a country of feudal nobles, peasants and unemployment his status as a workman was representative of a different world, a modern world, a world so concrete and real as to appear here almost impossible. He pointed out to me, from up above, the long stretch of dockyards, where he had lived and into which he had not been for so long. There had been a strike two days before, owing to the death of a workman, Giacomo Tricomi, who had been blown up at two in the morning by an explosion caused by a short circuit and thrown off the traveling crane in the factory, after working without interruption all day and all the evening. Conversation turned to the conditions of work in that very limited industrial area, and to Florio, founder of Sicilian industry, a unique modern middle-class figure, at war with a hostile social structure which got the better of him in the end and brought his undertakings (which still await a historian to recount them) to decay and ruin in the course of a single generation. And so we went on to talk of the Mafia, of the Mafia of today, renewed and enlarged beyond its traditional limits of the feudal estates into the world of business and trade and industry. The two young friends, S. and P., who were with us, were both of them, in different ways and with different interests, experts in the history and life of Sicily. And one of them in particular, the lawyer S.—tall, fair-haired, pleasant-looking—had perhaps, both owing to his professional activities and to his concrete ideals of reform, the most profound knowledge of anyone I came across on the subject of the origins and the meaning of the Mafia. The word "Mafia" was uttered, then (that word which yet sounds so mysterious in the ears of anyone who lives far away from here, a word that is frightening and romantic at the same time, a word that evades both knowledge and definition)—that word was uttered just as we had climbed the hill above the broad garden-filled valley of the Conca d'Oro and were entering the piazza of Monreale. The hot African wind was blowing with a scorching breath that made the green palm-fountain, with its mossy, grooved, Saracen stonework, in the retired corner of the cloister, seem, to our imagination, even fresher and moister than it was. But we were not intending to stop and contemplate the cloister again, and the mosaics and the great Christ who is so severely remote. We had a long way to go. We halted just for a moment at the corner of the piazza in front of a kind of warehouse which opened on to the pavement: this had been the headquarters of a former political party. P., turning his sharp black eyes and his sharp profile hither and thither and indicating the piazza and the town with a wide sweep of his arm, said to me: "This is one of the capitals of the Mafia; from here you can dominate Palermo." And pointing his finger at the open warehouse, where an old mustachioed custodian was sitting on a chair at the door, he added with a laugh: "And this is one of its central offices, though by no means the only one." There was no one in this office, nothing but shabby billiard-tables, one of which was for table football, with things like spoons made of magnetic metal, in which our imagination, influenced by the subject under discussion, could picture the balls firmly caught and forever inextricable. Then I recalled and related to my friends an old jocular epigram which was going the rounds in 1944, and which said:

DANS LE PLI DE L'ÉTENDARD
ATTENTION: LES CAGOULARDS!

It was the time of the Liberation committees: the author, I think, was considering (with how much foundation, I don't know) that his illustrious and extremely honest and noble and respectable Liberal friends were the innocent standard bearers of an army of an entirely different nature.

Monreale was now behind us; the road goes uphill, the mountains widen out all round and become desolate, the slopes are rugged and covered with stones. We were coming into the bandit country, into the gloomy realm of Giuliano. On our right rose the mountain country, solitary and precipitous, on our left the eye wandered over more and more deserted expanses towards Altofonte and the remote Piana degli Albanesi, and Portella della Paglia from which you go down to San Giuseppe Jato—names that by their very sound awaken an echo of memories, even in those who do not recall the detailed story of ambush and slaughter, in the same way (though by different means) as places of mythological or heroic fame. Everything seems obscure as night and intricate as a forest in this very recent story of bandits (it is a story of only yesterday and yet it already echoes remotely in the mind, like the deeds of another period and another civilization; yet it is still actual to us today and sums up, in dramatic and revealing perspective, a great deal of Italy's present history), of their rise and their blossoming, of their relations, whether of alliance or rupture, with the Mafia, of the contacts, both of the one and the other, with the police and the government institutions and the political parties, of the actions of the government and of the local authorities, of the popular reaction: everything is obscure and intricate like the bare gorges in these mountains; and thought becomes confused, and would prefer to shun the whole problem, if it were not for a thread which helps it to find its way, like a patrol sent out in advance to reconnoitre in a mapless, roadless country, among traps and snares. Mafia and bandits are not, as they might seem, a curiosity, a phenomenon without roots, a sudden, fortuitous

155

sickness, nor yet one derived from singular racial characteristics; but they exist, so to speak, in a crack or cleft in a land without continuity, hidden from eyes that are used to order and the ordinary, to the softening of contours and colors. They are embedded in a fold of history which many, all too many, banners seek to conceal.

"This land," said S., as the car struggled up the deserted mountainsides, "has always been a land of invasions and conquests: all the invaders and conquerors were foreigners, and remained so. They came, they took, and they went away again, creating and leaving behind them, to rule the country, their own representatives, nobles, princes, dukes and barons, an aristocracy of foreign origin and, like all aristocracies, naturally at loggerheads with the distant government; they also left military forces insufficient for any purpose beyond keeping possession of the land and preserving respect for the barons. There was therefore lacking—there has always lacked, and there still lacks—an intermediate class: between the peasant population and the foreign government there has always been an abyss, a cleft; and it is here that the Mafia lies hidden. To reach the great expanses of the feudal estates, the villages of the interior, the land, the peasants, to get the taxes paid, to squeeze out the fat of the land, so necessary for distant governments and for the life of the nobles—for all this there have never been sufficient forces nor yet direct agreements; the whole life of the island has always been left to its own devices. Hence the excise officer, and the field guard, the superintendent who not merely ensures the exaction of property to his own advantage but also takes the place of the absent government in all functions of order and justice, who puts his own code of honor in place of a foreign, impotent law, and becomes, gradually, an absolute and solitary power, supported by prestige and absence. This is the historical origin of the Mafia: hence comes the tacit, fundamental pact of impunity between the Mafia and the government. As long as the government is foreign and maintains its foreign quality, as long as it fails to derive directly from the population and their everyday life, so long is the Mafia necessary to it, as its sole means of preservation. And when the bandit, that popular hero of revolt against the government, makes his appearance in the woods, it will again be the Mafia which makes use of him to conduct its own bloody affairs, without his becoming aware of it, using him as a tool for its own ends, for its continual blackmail of the authorities, and making him a bargaining point for threats and scandal; and the authorities, in their turn, put up a pretense of struggle and war against both the bandits and the Mafia, avoiding the only method which would lead, bloodlessly, to their disappearance.

"It is an old story: it has always been like that, more or less. Do you know the tale of *Pippinu u Lombardu*, Peppino the Lombard, who was a sort of Pisciotta of his time? Some days ago, as I was skimming through some papers at the Storia Patria Library, I actually came across the original documents of his trial, which was in 1860. Don Peppino was a schoolmaster from Milan, who came down to Sicily to exercise his profession here, amongst people who, being almost entirely illiterate, might have provided him with a great number of customers, even among the highly placed and well to do. However, when he arrived here and came into contact with the bandits, he considered it would be more to his advantage to join up with them, and, in quite a short time, having considerable authority as an educated man, and also being not without aptitude, ended by becoming the chief of the band—of a band which achieved a great reputation. Now, as you can imagine, it is precisely this matter of excessive reputation which forces the police to interfere in matters which otherwise they would be happy to disregard and so it was in this case; so that soon Peppino the Lombard found himself in prison with a large number of his men, and was brought to trial. It was just at this point that the papers became really interesting: for what happened at the trial was that Peppino the Lombard, relying for his own safety upon this expedient, and not being bound (he being a foreigner) by ties of loyalty to his fellows, "talked" without reserve, revealing the bonds of understanding there had been between his band and the police and the authorities. The papers do not say what the end of the matter was: certainly Peppino was both cleverer and luckier than Pisciotta: there is no mention, in his case, of poisoned coffee; nor is there any allusion to promotions and honors for those who had relations with him. This is an old story, and it may interest you as an anecdote. But the background of the whole question remains the same. These mountains are the same: the feudal estates are the same. You know, partly at any rate, the story of Giuliano. That, truly, is a story which provides an example. If you don't touch the feudal estates, if you preserve the existing poverty, if the government does not become a peasants' government, the bandit will always be there, in those mountains (and in the towns, too, and in the palaces of Palermo), and the Mafia will be there too, and accounts will have to be settled with it —and it, naturally, is bound to win—and the ministers in Rome will have to come to an agreement with its representatives, both great and small, and the *carabinieri* will be sent out to die on the roads, a death as cruel as it is useless. The banditry of the period since the war could have been stamped out without a single death and without spending a penny—ever since the time of the separatist armies. General Branca realized this very well; he saw clearly, and he spoke clearly in his report. But in Rome, of course, they couldn't pay any attention to him, because you can't serve two masters and do two contradictory things at the same time. So things have gone on as they were, in this tragic and at the same time grotesque way, which may perhaps seem almost incomprehensible to you, and with this epic tale of subterfuges and pretenses, of lies and false actions, which would seem absurd and unreal if they were not documented by so much blood and so much money. D'you see that

159

house? It's the house of a priest from Pioppo. It appears almost certain now that that is where Giuliano was killed."

We stopped a moment to look. It was a small two story house at a bend in the road just before a little bridge; it was painted yellow and purple with a colored key-pattern round the edges of the walls. A cement staircase at one side led to the upper floor, and the façade had a balcony adorned with the letters N.S.—for *Nostro Signore,* Our Lord. Looking down from the balcony was a girl with long black tresses and black eyes and a made-up face, wearing a bright-colored dressing-gown; and another one, also dark and made up, came out and watched us as we drove off.

The road rose and fell, in short ups and downs, among poorly cultivated fields and rocks. For years, my companions told me, the land hereabouts was entirely abandoned and the peasants remained in the villages, not daring to go into the fields, from terror, not so much of the bandits, as of the police drag nets. We went past the houses in Sagana where, they told me, Giuliano's meetings with inspectors of police took place, and past the new bridge. Here begins— and continues for some miles—a most horrific, savage gorge between the slopes of Monte Signora on the left and those of Monte Gibilmesi on the right, in a fierce landscape that breathes of traps and ambushes at every step, and in its shaggy loneliness is the very image of fear. Rocks of odd and violent shape bestrew the naked slopes in myriads, rocks slanting and crooked and pointed, rained down, as it were, from heaven, scattered all about by a malign, baleful power, beneath a desert sun.

We went down in silence, now, under the spell of a nature that seemed fired with a dumb fury. Montelepre appeared on our right, halfway up the side of its savage mountain. After we had passed Borgetto, we soon reached Partinico, facing the great plain with its innumerable gardens stretching away to the distant sea. The streets were full of people in their holiday clothes, under the burning sun. They were walking up and down, going to Mass in the church on the piazza, beside the fountain which is embellished with a reproachful Latin inscription. We stopped for a moment for a cup of coffee in an extremely modern bar full of scintillating machines. The girl at the cash desk compelled our admiration, so great was the beauty of her sparkling eyes, of her lips, of her skin of golden earth-color. Two young men were leaning against the bar in front of their glasses; they had ordered two whiskies, but could not make up their minds to drink them.

"I'm going to drink my whisky," said one.

"A pity not to," answered the other.

"Your health."

"Your health."

At the door of the bar an old man sold us a packet of roasted seeds, beans and chick-peas, and we left, scrunching these hard and unyielding vegetables between our teeth. We should be seeing Partinico again on our return, with its squalid quarters of half-starved people and other quarters where a large proportion of the male inhabitants are in prison.

As we drove along the splendid road, S. and P. and Alfio resumed their previous conversation. And they described life at Partinico during the years of Giuliano and explained to me the recent changes in the activity of the Mafia since the reform laws came into force, which aim at breaking up the feudal estates and reducing the function of the excise officers—how this activity, in fact, is veering, in an up-to-date manner, toward business, toward industry and commerce and local government contracts, toward political and industrial affairs, though it still has not given up its traditional, fierce defense of the feudal system; and how that is the point where the peasant movement rises to its greatest intensity, as was shown by the recent criminal incident, the killing of a peasant trade unionist, Salvatore Carnevale, a few weeks ago, at Sciara. They spoke with great emotion of this recent event, of the dead man, of his mother, of his village, so that I, who had already heard of it, suggested going to Sciara later. In the meantime we had arrived at Alcamo. We searched in vain for a statue of Ciullo d'Alcamo—in vain, for, odd to relate, it does not exist. We had a bet on it, and went to ask about it at a butcher's shop in the piazza. They knew nothing of it: they advised us to try at the druggist's shop opposite. A tall, sturdy priest in a dirty, greasy, torn gown, with a brutal face, two little eyes beneath shaggy, bushy eyebrows, an apelike forehead, and a coarse, fierce-lipped mouth, who was buying a piece of meat covered with flies, threw us a glance of such suspicion that it was positively frightening. The old druggist explained to us that the statue had always been planned, and that perhaps some day the plan would be put into execution. The church at the far end of the piazza was like a gray table against the sky.

The silence of the open country came down upon us again as we passed through mountains of strange outline and deep color toward Calatafimi; and then, in the midst of a great shell-like hollow surrounded by yellow mountains and covered to the horizon on every side in a mantle of golden stubble, where, as far as the eye can reach, there is neither house, nor tree, nor human being to be seen, we caught sight suddenly of the Temple of Segesta. It is of the same color as gold, as corn, as the mysterious, lonely earth upon which it stands, yet at the same time it has a rosy flush like a human or divine body; it is, as it were, a harmonic, eternally serene translation of the tragic nature around it, transforming, in its perfect simplicity, an endless story, and even the very presence of the Gods, into an architectural formula, into a number, forcing us to think poetically in numbers, and to rest, motionless and satisfied, in the mellow rhythm of that elementary formula, where lizards run and the sunshine splinters the shadows.

It is a long road to Trapani and Mount Eryx, with no villages, only a few nameless clusters of cottages at the roadside, until Paparella and the first marvelous glimpse from the steep hill, of the most ancient of seas as it appeared between the tunny pickling factory at Bonagía and far-off Cape San Vito. At each curve it seemed as though the world of struggle and hardship, of color and poverty through which we had passed was being left behind by far more than the few yards we had covered, was receding in space and time as we climbed up among the strange mythological mists that so thickly envelop this isolated mountain and seem to enclose it and detach it from all else. Down below gleamed the salt mines of Trapani, and the islands looked like ships ready to sail.

Everyone has heard of or has seen this medieval town of gray stone, with its streets that are paved with decorated slabs and its trim, flower-filled courtyards, this Assisi of the South, full of churches and convents and silent streets and of an extraordinary accumulation of mythological memories. Father Castelnuovo, who wrote a rare and highly learned history of the place, traces back the vicissitudes of his native town, in pages that are moreover quite charming, to the very dawn of time—as indeed do all the local scholars. Here came the Cyclops and the Sicanians, to this city founded by Eryx, son of Venus, who met his death at the hand of Heracles, a hero who, like Garibaldi, stopped everywhere; here came Aeneas, brother of Eryx on the mother's side, here the Phoenicians, the Carthaginians and the Romans, and so many others afterwards; here was the famous temple of Venus, *"Erycina ridens,"* and the anagogic and catagogic feasts of the departure and return of the doves, and so on. And surely these legends and stories are all true, in places like this, where time condenses with the hardness of a crystal.

We wished to taste the famous almond paste confectionery made by the nuns of an enclosed order in a convent here. Going into the hall, we made known our desires to a vague shadow behind the double grating, and a moment later, without a word being spoken, the sweets appeared in the turning-box—delicate green and pink and violet and blue flowers—and we left the money in their place. A whispering voice inquired whether we also wanted some rugs; and the rugs came out through the turning-box and the ceremony of exchange was repeated. These rugs are made of rags, in very beautiful colors and Saracen designs.

We wandered, as though out of this world, through silent streets where you meet no one except an occasional old woman wrapped in a black shawl, where you see no children, nor even a speck of dust; then went into the principal church:

QUESTO TEMPIO

ONDE L'UMANO SAPERE

ORACOLEGGIAVA

RESTARNE I SOLI RUDERI A MONUMENTO

O COMPITO DELLE FUTURE GENERAZIONI

APPENA SEI ANNI

DALL'IMMORTALE ARCIPRETE AGUGLIANO

PER LA SPESA DI LIRE CENTO MILLE

INGENTE

RIGUARDATO IL REDDITO E LA CONDIZIONE DEI TEMPI

165

IL 20 AGOSTO 1865
IN SI LEGGIADRE GOTICHE FORME
APRIVASI AL PUBBLICO CULTO
FRA L'ENTUSIASMO DI IMMENSO POPOLO

IDDIO
LE CURE DELL'IMPAVIDO PASTORE
LA PIETÀ DEI FEDELI E PIU DEI BORGHESI
COMPIRONO
UN TANTO MIRACOLO.*

Some young men in the piazza recognized me and took me to see the library and the museum. Here lives the ancient Monsignore Antonino Amico, the Eryx librarian. He is eighty years old and almost blind, but he still carries on his life work—research, archives, collation of old papers, transcription of documents—so that he will leave scholars a mass of precious material for the history of Sicily. His appearance is appropriate to his work—the bent, lean body, the luminous glance in the wizened, rare, venerable face, different, like Mount Eryx, from everything that surrounds it; he might well be a contemporary of those nebulous figures, Saturn, the Cyclops, Butes and the "Venus Erycina."

* (Free translation): Of this temple, whence human wisdom spoke in oracles, there remained only the ruins as a monument or as a task for future generations. In barely six years, and with the expenditure of a hundred thousand lire—a huge sum, considering the revenue and the state of the times—the church was reopened for public worship by the immortal Archpriest Agugliano on August 20th, 1865, in its graceful Gothic form, amid the enthusiasm of an immense multitude. Almighty God, the diligence of the intrepid pastor, the piety of the faithful and of the many yeomen of the neighborhood accomplished this great miracle.

Having come back to the seashore and the strange company of our own contemporaries, we now drove through Castellammare del Golfo, which lies spread out like a gray, open fan, past the scattered villas of Alcamo Marina and the sand dunes of Balestrate, toward Trappeto and Borgo di Dio, the goal of today's journey. We had come to see Danilo Dolci, the architect from Trieste who, after two years' experience at Nomadelfia, has established his life and his work here, among the poor of this village of fishermen and peasants. As we came into it, the place—owing, perhaps, to its being the hottest hour of the day—appeared uninhabited. At last a woman looked out of a doorway and we asked her for him, and then went on, according to her instructions, past the railway, up a steep, stony street, to a kind of large, stone-built shed, of recent construction, which we thought was his house. There was no one here, either; we looked in at a window and saw that the inside was a single large, empty room, its walls all decorated with huge line drawings in pencil or charcoal on the white ground of the wall itself, all of them representing, with a childish minuteness and an elegant accuracy and precision, the grasses and flowers of the meadows. A stonemason who was going past on his way to another, not yet finished, building close by, told us that this was the "university," where meetings were held and lectures given, that the house on which he was now working would be the office of the Irrigation Society, and that Dolci lived lower down.

Up there, at the noonday hour, a wide and enchanting landscape opened out in front of us. The ground on which we stood was scorched by the sun, but out of it—the fruit, evidently, of loving care— sprang tomatoes and green vegetables. Behind us were the cruel mountains we had passed through that morning, and Montelepre, softened by distance, on the far side of the plain of Partinico; in front of us a serene, untouched sea and the coast stretching away toward Palermo, full of blue, unexplored caves. It seemed a happy country, fed by a friendly sun. We went into Danilo's house and he welcomed us in a friendly, open manner; he is tall, robust, with a big, well-formed, Nordic head, and lively eyes behind his glasses; cheerful and full of internal energy, always alert and prepared, as can be seen even in his smallest movements, for action. His house is modest and bare, with a piano, a desk covered with plans and papers; and the white wall is adorned, like the one at the university, with an enormous design of grasses and leaves, the work, like the others, of his boy pupils. He at once began talking to us of the work that lies so near to his heart, of the irrigation project for the whole area which will bring about a profound change in the situation and combat the extreme poverty. He also explained all his other enterprises, the crèche, the school, the assistance organization, the war against abuse of fishing rights, and the investigations, and the studies and lectures and concerts—in fact, all the activities which we knew of from his writings, but which here presented themselves to our eyes in their right proportions. His was not the tone of the pure missionary or the philanthropist, but that of a man who has confidence, who has confidence in others (a general confidence in humanity), who arouses confidence around him and feels that, with this weapon alone, he can make life gradually spring up, by spontaneous force, in a place where it would seem impossible; who from sheer confidence, has installed himself, almost by chance and by no special choice, in one of the many thousand desperately poor villages, and has resolved to take root there, sharing other people's lives in every way and burning his boats behind him in order *not* to be the philanthropist who arrives from outside and who, whatever he may do, remains an outsider. Danilo introduced us to his wife, a widow from Trappeto with five children; and other children were coming and wandering about the room: and in them and in his wife, and in the young mistress of the infants' school, and in the builders and everyone else there was the same look of cheerfulness and activity, as though nothing, in their situation, could appear strange. We knew of his long-sustained struggles, of the obtuse hostility and mistrust on the part of the authorities, so similar to that of the realistic, prudent tsarist police and bureaucracy in relation to the utopian, idealistic Russian populists. Dolci did not speak of all this; instead, he described to us the terrible conditions in Trappeto and Partinico, which he knows house by house, family by family—the diseases, the illiteracy, the delinquency, the prostitution, mortal effects of an age-long poverty and distress, and sole origin, according to him, of banditry and of other evils deliberately preserved by a government policy which refuses to clear them up and which wastes thousands of millions of lire on police repression of banditry, where millions would suffice to abolish its causes. He showed us his statistics of bandits' families, where hunger, illiteracy and unemployment are constant characteristics, in villages where the majority of the population are, as they call them here, "industrials"—that is, men who work industriously, without either land or a trade, or the possibility of ever having land or a trade in order to earn a living and keep themselves alive. These things are known to anybody who wishes to know them, but Danilo was anxious to show them to us in real life: real things speak far more clearly than words and statistics. We went down with him to the *Vallone,* through wretched, stinking streets; we went into houses without floors, full of flies and putrid wetness, and saw, once again, as in so many other villages and districts of the South, the gray face of misery—men without work, demoralized, with no will or desire left, mothers without milk, children undernourished and reduced to skeletons. In Via Silvio Pellico, a kind of precipitous ravine between tumbledown hovels, I saw, opposite the house in which a famous bandit was hidden during these last years, a room—like all the others, a dark den—in which lives one of the young men who have been attracted here by Dolci's example, a musician from Geneva who goes fishing with the fishermen upon a sea that has been reduced

170

to sterility and emptiness by the piracy of poachers—a piracy benevolently tolerated by the authorities. A little farther up, a man still young, haggard in the face and shivering with tuberculosis, was trying, wrapped in a woolen shawl, to warm himself in the sun. In the midst of that utter destitution, eyes nevertheless looked at Danilo with a gleam of hope; and it seemed to me that I could see reflected in them a certain vague hope even in themselves.

We found the same signs of the birth of hope in thick darkness on the faces of the poor people of Partinico, where Danilo also volunteered to accompany us. It was again the usual, tragically monotonous spectacle of misery, perhaps even sadder here because this was a *town* misery and there was therefore about it a greater sense of loneliness and abandonment; it varied strangely in the different quarters of the town, even though they were only a few steps away from one another. There is a district called Madonna behind the old town hall, with its great empty piazza, which is the district of the bandits, where a large proportion of the men are in prison, and suspicion and pride and fierce protest can be felt in the very air, in the constrained expression on the women's faces, in the closed doors, the empty streets. It is the cowherds' quarter; and they are men full of energy who are urged on by their very virtues to answer offense with violence, to resist in the most elementary manner, to go with Giuliano in order to live. The Spine Sante quarter is more squalid; this consists of a few streets higher up, a few steps from the church and from the café where we had stopped that morning. Clouds of children, emaciated but very beautiful, welcomed Dolci as he passed, calling him by name: "Danine, Danine!"—happy to pronounce that name, as though they were uttering a magic formula. We went with him into all the houses and everywhere we encountered the most elementary problems of a world slavishly confined within the limits set by hunger and disease; and once again, as had happened so many years before, I was forced against my will to recall old and almost forgotten notions of medicine. In Spine Sante the answer to the offense of the outside world is not banditry but—feebler and more painful—disease and madness. Here too the streets are dusty and dirty, but in the dirt there are no remains of food to be seen, no orange peel, no leaves, no cabbage stalks, no tins, no bones: the lean dogs sniff round with an air of disappointment. There live, in only a few houses, no less than seventeen declared cases of mental disease, and goodness knows how many others less evident and less clamorous. There was a young man sitting motionless in a chair: his old mother showed him to us and tried in vain to rouse him to speech; his apathetic, schizophrenic silence had lasted for years. In a doorway stood another young man, thin-faced, dim-eyed, his arms dangling at this sides—quite quiet at the moment, but, his neighbors told us, when attacked by hunger, a raging madman. We went into another house where we saw a man shut up in a cage. The little room in which the whole family lived had been divided by a row of iron bars like those used for wild animals, and inside the cage a young man with a bestial face and terrible black eyes was pacing up and down. In the house next door the head of the family had been lying in bed, without moving, for months, shut off from the world, filled with some dark anguish of his own, almost nonexistent. He let us come close to the bed and then covered his face with the sheet like a dead man.

Night was coming on, and we left for Palermo. The piazza at Mondello was twinkling with lights, with fish stalls all along the shore. The warm, soft air was full of the smell of seaweed and of the so-called *quaglie* or "quails"—eggplant fried and slit up into flowerlike shapes with a hundred petals—and of polyps thrown into great cauldrons to boil, to be taken out later, hot, violet-colored, curling, and cut up on the counter, showing the pure whiteness of their insides and the baroque volutes of their tentacles. From great wicker baskets plunged into the sea were brought mountains of sea urchins which were opened by the fishermen with a single highly skillful stroke of the knife to reveal the sulphur and iodine yellow of their entrails.

"It's hard work," said the young fisherman who was opening them with such extraordinary grace.

"You can't earn enough to live on. No, they're not found here, you have to go to Capo Gallo, or all the

173

way to Capo San Vito; it takes a day to get there in a boat, and a day to come back, and if the sea's bad you don't catch anything. Sometimes it's all right, sometimes there are a few dozen, but we still go hungry."

4

"When I was a boy I used to eat sea urchins whole, rind and spines and shell and all, I was so hungry— for our mouths get to be like millstones. And I used to eat prickly pears, too, skins and all, and they didn't do me any harm, I was so hungry—for our stomachs are like cauldrons and down below the throat there's a blazing heat that burns up everything." These words were addressed to me by the broom maker of Aspra, as he opened some sea urchins which he had gone to catch for me among the rocks on the stretch of coast between Bagheria and Cape Zafferano, beneath the ruins of the ancient city of Soluntum; it is perhaps the most beautiful place that can be found anywhere for a human body to lie in the sun. Steep rocks end, at the sea's edge, in a kind of shelf or pedestal of stone just above the level of the water, which, rising and falling gently, covers it from time to time; and this shelf, full of seaweed and shells and madrepores and sea creatures, where you can walk hidden from sight by the rocks which overhang and are hollowed out below water level into endless invisible intricacies, is pierced here and there by large round or heart-shaped holes, like little lakes or natural baths, carpeted with soft seaweed and filled with scarcely-moving water. Here, in one of these marine hearts, you can lie down flat while unexpected shower baths spray up in sudden jets from holes in the rock, with subterranean gurglings; and there you can linger, dallying without thought, tenderly enveloped by the sea, with nothing visible but the impenetrable blue.

The broom maker's hut is up above the rocks, and here you can lie and get dry on a soft bed of piled-up rushes, while he weaves others into triple brooms that look like three-plumed crests of paladins or savage warriors; they cost seventy lire. I was told of this paradisal spot by the duchess of S., mother of a woman friend of mine, who, hearing that I was passing through Bagheria, had conveyed an invitation to me to go up to her villa because she was extremely anxious to meet me; so, having found the cart shop of the Brothers Ducati closed (temporarily closed because work is getting scarcer even for those who are the best painters anywhere on this coast, and because the number of carts is decreasing month by month and they are being gradually replaced by trucks), I went up to the villa, which is marvelous both in architecture and in its gardens, high above the village and looking out over the sea. Here the wedding feast of one of the maids was going on, with a flight of birds out of the nuptial pie, and dancing, and a dinner consisting, according to custom, of a single dish of macaroni *al forno* with a ragout of meat, followed immediately by sweetmeats, tarts, almond cake, fritters, gaily-colored puddings, maca-roons, *africanelli, pavesini, svizzeri,* and an endless quantity of ice puddings, *cassate, bombes* Ethiopia, moka cream, hazel nuts Chantilly, and preserved strawberries. The duchess presided with good-na-tured authority in the midst of the feast; she took me over the villa, which is full of bizarre statues by Ximenes—a souvenir of nineteenth century interna-tional exhibitions—and showed me her own room in which she lives remote from the world, which, she says, she hates. She was once a beauty, and I believe many hearts have throbbed for her, and one can still see the clear record of it in her face; and she is full of vital energy and a strange sort of violence. With this energy and violence of hers she assailed me with questions. For a very long time, she told me, she had wanted to know whether I was better or worse than my books; and I had to submit—with what result, I do not know—to comparisons and examinations that took every possible point into consideration and that moved from literature to painting, and even to love, and to God. How could one resist this unfettered force of nature? She made me promise that for good or ill, one way or another, I would write something about her with complete sincerity: and I, all too briefly, am fulfilling my promise. Before she dis-missed me we were joined by a young prince, whether her friend or relation I do not know, who related fantastic extravagances and follies on the part of certain spectacular members of his family—figures only recently dead, of impressive stature and with imposing beards, who had been full of feudal haughtiness, of inordinate manias, of insolent, crazy vitality. Adventures, jests, mystifications, disguises, all of them with a grain of genius and madness in them; and with a feeling for life as though it were a theater with no limits. At one moment the conversation turned to Sciara, where he had spent long periods of his childhood at the castle of a relation of his, Princess Notarbartolo. I told him of my intention to go there, and of the killing of the peasants' leader. He had no precise knowledge of it, he vaguely thought he had heard it spoken of: the man must have been a violent, hotheaded character. . . . "Sciara," he said to me, "Sciara is a prosperous village; there is work, there are cattle, there are no poor people, it's a wonderful place for shooting, the country is full of quails. As a boy I used to stay up at the castle, I know all the people in Sciara; we used to go up and shoot on Monte San Calogero, we used to get quails there, and once we killed a golden eagle."

Here I was, then, today, on the road to Sciara with Alfio and his Appia car, driving along the coast road once again, after four years, in the blazing July sun. Having passed Porticello and Casteldaccia, and Altavilla Milicia, white on its hill, and San Nicolò, we had to stop for a long time at the Trabia level crossing, which is perpetually closed because of work on the double line and for the shunting of trains. A small boy came and offered us a basket of freshly picked strawberries. We discussed the price, and Alfio, well used to seeing this boy who took advantage of the enforced stop at the level crossing to ply his trade, asked him, in a casual sort of way so as to make him talk, how the dispute with his rivals had gone. This imaginary dispute, it turned out, had really taken place, and the boy had settled it to his own advantage by a spontaneous application of the rule of force and prestige which governs the whole country. "I've taken a partner," he said. "That other chap wanted to sell strawberries here, where I have the right to, and he was bigger than me, but now that there are two of us we are in control and he has given up coming here."

The road beyond Trabia and Termini Imerese is the same as the road to Isnello as far as a fork leading off to the right. Here one leaves the coast and climbs up a very rough, dusty road, full of holes, toward the interior. The look of the country changes at once. A great valley opens out between bare mountains, and far away on the opposite mountain Cerda comes into sight, gray amid a naked expanse of fields and surrounded by that same color of earth and stubble, that same air of silence and of long-established malaria which seems always to accompany the toil of the peasants like a continuous, pathetic musical note. On the right Monte San Calogero rises to a great height, towering in its loneliness, its peak wrapped in clouds.

From its interior hot thermal waters flow down to the sea. Underneath Sicily, so they relate, lies forever a Cyclops, crushed beneath the land's great weight, through the vengeance of the gods. His mouth is beneath Etna and hurls forth flames of lava; his shoulders are at Syracuse and the Straits, his feet are underneath Mount Eryx, and underneath Monte San Calogero are his loins, distilling, forever, these beneficial waters.

The road winds uphill like a corkscrew, between the stubble fields of the feudal estate. We came into an olive grove of huge, venerable trees, twisted and gray and silver against the yellow of the stubble. This was an olive grove belonging to the princess, as indeed does all the surrounding land. "Here," said Alfio, "over these olives, Salvatore Carnevale's first action was taken. Over these olives and this corn. When he was killed, the corn was high . . ." Now, the corn had been harvested; here and there, in the distance, in the open expanses of the estate, there were straw-stacks like square towers, and the gray shadow of the big olive trees lay spread over the ground.

"I knew Salvatore Carnevale," went on Alfio; "I saw him very often when he was alive, here at Sciara, and at the peasants' meetings. He was thirty-two, tall and dark-skinned, with black eyes and hair, full of fire and energy. He was a good speaker, too: decided, violent, uncompromising, but at the same time very well-balanced and with a precise and straightforward view of things. He was one of the very best, a real peasant leader. He was the only one of that quality here at Sciara, and the others understood that perfectly well. It was he who founded the Sciara Socialist Club, in 1951, and who got the Labor Exchange started. There had never been anything at Sciara—no Party, no organization for the *contadini*, nothing at all. It was just a feudal village, as you'll see. It had been firmly stuck in exactly the same conditions for goodness knows how many centuries—a feudal estate, with the princess, the superintendents, the field guards; and the laborers, who hardly even knew they existed, absolutely unchanged for centuries. It's a terribly poor village, and of course (though they'll tell you it's not true) in the hands of the Mafia. It's not a big Mafia center like Caccamo, Termini or Trabia or Cerda which lie all round it, because it's quite a small place. But those few members of the Mafia are its masters, and they lay down the law. That's the elementary situation of feudal estate villages. Carnevale was the first to take any action, and his example and his courage set everything in motion. For he had a clear mind, and understood it was no use coming to agreements, that the peasants must move with their own forces, and that, in order to live, they must break with the old feudal structure and must not allow any half-measures nor accept even the smallest compromise. He realized that intransigence is not so much a moral duty as a necessity of life, and that the first step is organization, and that support and help can come only from organizations that have nothing to do with

181

existing powers. That was why he might sometimes appear extravagant, an extremist. He had realized that, in these primitive, strained conditions, faced by an organized power whose ramifications reach everywhere, which controls everything by its own laws, the essential thing is not to allow oneself to be seduced or bribed; and never to accept, as real things, either fear, or loyalty, or the rule of terror. He paid for it with his life. But the village has changed, as you will see.

"On this very spot, these olives belonging to the princess gave him his first victory, and perhaps they also condemned him to death. According to ancient custom, the peasants of Sciara who sowed the corn in the olive grove took no share in the gathering of the olives. The corn was divided up in the old-established proportions. The olives belonged entirely to the owner, who entrusted the picking of them to people from outside, to farm laborers and harvesters from Caccamo and their superintendents. Carnevale, taking his stand on the law, demanded that the gathering of the olives should be entrusted to the same peasants who grew the corn, and that the division should be made as the law lays down, so that the peasants' share should be sixty per cent and the princess' forty. It was the first organized peasant movement. One of the managers of the estate at once offered Carnevale all the olives he wanted, if he gave up the struggle. The peasants won, they obtained almost everything they demanded; the Mafia was offended and stricken to its very foundations—

182

in its prestige—not so much because of the trade union question in itself as because of the bold and intransigent way in which matters had been conducted. Shortly afterward the occupation of the land began. I think this was in October 1951. You know how these familiar, solemn ceremonies took place— with women and children and flags, all going, as though to a *festa,* to take symbolic possession of the land and then going back home again. Carnevale led them. They came up here, over these fields which are called the Giardinaccio section (that was where he was afterward killed). On its return to the village the procession was stopped by the police sergeant, and Carnevale and three other peasants were summoned to the town offices for discussions, then arrested and sent for eight days to the prison at Termini Imerese; and again, on this occasion too, there were threats and blandishments from the Mafia. A superintendent made overtures to Carnevale's mother, offering her the best holding of olive trees if her son would drop the whole game, and uttering obscure but quite obvious threats if she did not fall in with his suggestions. But she herself will tell you about all these things far better than I can."

The olive grove came to an end and there was open ground again, with harvested corn as far as the eye could reach, as far, in fact, as a distant hump beyond which, all of a sudden, the village came into view. To tell the truth, the village itself was not visible, but the castle, high on a rock, and down below it the church, had appeared, as though they had sprung up out of the earth. Between the castle and the church lay the village, out of sight. It looked like a heraldic picture of feudal Sicily, too simplified, too symbolic to be real, with just those two black vertical outlines cut out against the sky, the symbols of power —the former taller and more arrogant, the latter subdued but sharp, and, in the middle, almost nonexistent, in their hovels that seem to mingle with the earth, the peasants.

A waterless valley opened like a cleft in the burnt dust of the fields, over toward the hill where Carnevale had been killed. We left the car and started climbing up the slope. We came to a vegetable garden and a little cottage: four small mongrel dogs ran out at us, barking furiously, and the *contadino* himself appeared in the doorway, looking suspiciously at us. But when he saw which way our steps were taking us, he gave us a greeting, and, pointing with a princely gesture to the four small fruit trees in his garden, told us to pick all we wanted, that it was ours. We went up through thistles and prickly grasses until, higher up, we came into corn again and at last reached a horizontal path, visible a long way off, on that flat ground, owing to an upright stone landmark. It was here that Carnevale died. The stone records it with a simple inscription, two words of which, however—and those the most modest and innocent, expressing the grief of the whole population—can only be read through a covering layer of whitewash; they were effaced by order of the prefect.

The corn is cut now and the eye can see far along the path which leads from Sciara—half an hour's walk from here—to the stone quarry where Carnevale worked. But when, at dawn on the sixteenth of May, his murderers waited for him here, the corn was high, and covered them. They must have stopped and waited for him here for a long time; you can still see traces of footmarks here and there on the ground above the path. And they idled away this hour of waiting, before they shot him, by eating beans; there are still dried-up pods lying about on the ground. These bean pods speak malignantly, I think, like ancient ruins with marks of fire upon them, or old, yellowed documents. Thus do things change their nature and become proofs of real happenings, full of meaning, whether good or evil; no longer mere objects, but witnesses, participants. I stooped and picked up one of these pods. Some peasants who had seen us beside the stone came down from the fields, like birds who discern their prey from afar and swoop suddenly down, or swift-moving inhabitants of the desert. They halted respectfully a few steps away from us and greeted us without asking who we were: "Good day, comrades."

"Carnevale is the last, so far," said Alfio, "of the peasants to be killed on the feudal estates by the Mafia. The list in these recent years has been a long one, as you know. He had been away from here for two years, working at Montevarchi. When he came back, the land reform had begun. Seven hundred hectares had been marked off for distribution, but only two hundred had been distributed, and those to whom land was assigned had had a series of 'notifications' from the Mafia warning them that they must not think they were going to enjoy with impunity the land they received. They had their haystacks burned, their gates broken down, their cattle or their goats or their plows stolen. The Mafia and the feudal estates defend themselves with even greater violence if the battle is already lost. As soon as he came back, Carnevale started again with the occupying of the land, so as to get legal measures applied: and for this he was tried and found guilty. Later he worked on the making of the road between Sciara and Caccamo, and then at the stone quarry for the construction of the double railway line between Termini and Trabia; that was what held us up at the level crossing. The quarry up above here, in the Giardinaccio, also belongs to the princess, and the work is carried out by a company from Bologna; but the people who run the whole thing are the local contractors in league with the Mafia. Carnevale was secretary of the construction workers, and demanded the eight-hour day laid down by contract—whereas they were working eleven hours—and also the payment of arrears of wages. He wrote to Palermo, held meetings attacking the Mafia, was again threatened and finally killed as he was going to work. The murder was signed and sealed, so to speak, with the usual symbols of Mafia killings—the facial wounds to disfigure the corpse, in sign of contempt; and the following day the theft of forty hens, for the traditional banquet.

186

Everything might easily have ended in silence, as on all the other occasions. The authorities would have made a show of investigating; nobody would have said a word. As on all other such occasions, there would have been talk of a private crime, for personal reasons, or reasons of honor or interest or vengeance. But this time, for the first time in the history of Sicily, it was not like that. Salvatore's mother spoke out, explicitly denouncing the Mafia at the court in Palermo. It was a great thing to do, because it broke the importance of a law and a custom whose power was sacred. There has been truly a change. On the day of Carnevale's death the village was terrorized, no one dared to go and see the dead man, who had been left abandoned in the mortuary. But his mother's denunciation drove away their terror; they were all at the funeral, and they had a sense of solidarity, feeling that they were on the right road and, so to speak, at the center of the world."

We had retraced our steps down the hill; once we had reached the road, we were in Sciara in a few minutes. A street goes right through it from one end to the other, going first up and then down again, and interrupted in the middle by a piazza with an eagle-crowned monument to the fallen and an absurd church of Dutch imitation Gothic style which has taken the place of the ancient church. From this street the wide, steep, stony side streets, like torrent beds, go up toward the castle and down toward the valley. They are *sciare,* they are bands or rivers of

187

stone rushing headlong down. As you climb up them, among goats and donkeys and cows, between the low stone hovels, you see the castle where they all converge. Seen from close, it is a modest little castle, almost like a deserted, crumbling country house; but the lofty, perpendicular rock on which it is built and the thorny hedges of prickly pear which surround it give it a rapacious, military appearance as of an isolated, impregnable fortress, a place of cruel segregation and of disdain.

But what peace, up there! The open country descends gradually as far as the foot of cloud-wrapped Monte San Calogero, a solemn silence lies over the fields, an untouched, pastoral enchantment binds together trees and plants and rocks, the gold of the stubble, the blue distances, right up to the empty sky. As you look down from there, the whole surrounding countryside is like an open book and nothing is hidden from the eye. In the complete immobility of the fields, the slightest movement of a bird, of an animal, of a human being stands out with brilliant clearness. All the streets of Sciara, all the houses, all the doors of all the houses, all the steps leading up to the doors, all the people sitting on the steps—you can see them separately and distinctly, as in a great picture without shadows. Whoever lives here has no need of spokesmen or spies; by a mere glance, he commands all. He knows who goes in or out, who has gone to work and who has come back, who has lit his lamp and who has had his dinner, who has milked his cow and who has closed

188

his door. And anyone who lives down below, in those doorways and in those houses, feels upon him the eye of that bird of prey on its perch.

In one of these descending streets, one of these stony ravines that slope down to the valley, is the house of Salvatore Carnevale and his mother, Francesca Serio; it is in the lower part of the village, and you get to it from the main street down high, narrow flights of stone steps. At the door was an old man with a wrinkled, sunburned face and a faded hat on his head: being quite accustomed to visits, he motioned to us to go in. The house consisted of a single long, narrow room, its only light coming from the door, with a loft at its farther end, a brick oven for baking bread near the entrance, a few utensils against the bare, whitewashed wall, and a bed against the other wall, underneath the loft. Beside the bed, sitting in a chair, her head covered with a black shawl, all alone, was Francesca, the mother of Carnevale. She is a woman of about fifty, still youthful-looking in her slim figure and her general appearance, still beautiful, in fact, with her sharp black eyes, the brownish white of her skin, her black hair, her pale, thin lips, her tiny, sharp teeth, her long, expressive, speaking hands; but with a hard, dried-up, violent beauty, opaque as stone, pitiless, apparently inhuman. She asked Alfio whether I was a work mate or a friend, made us sit down near her, beside that white bed which had been Salvatore's; and then she began to speak. She spoke of the death and of the life of her son as though she were resuming a discourse that

189

had been interrupted for a moment by our entrance. She talked, she recounted episodes, she reasoned and discussed and accused, with extreme rapidity and precision, alternating dialect with Italian and detailed narration with the logic of interpretation; and she was simply and completely absorbed in this continuous, endless discourse, the whole of her, without reserve—her life as a peasant, her past as a woman deserted and then widowed, the work she had done for years, and the death of her son, and her loneliness, and her house, and Sciara, and Sicily, and the whole of life; all these were contained in that violent yet orderly flow of words. Nothing exists in her, nothing exists for her, except this trial over which she presides and which she carries through all by herself, sitting on her chair beside the bed: the trial of the feudal system, of the servile state of the peasants, the trial of the Mafia and of the government. She identifies herself absolutely with her trial and herself has all its qualities: she is sharp, watchful, suspicious, astute, skillful, imperious, implacable. That is what this woman has made of herself, in one day: tears are no longer tears but words, and words are stones. She speaks with the hardness and precision of a judicial inquiry, with a profound and absolute assurance, like one who has suddenly reached a firm point on which to take a stand, a certainty: and this certainty, which dries her tears and makes her ruthless, is justice itself. True justice, that is; justice as the realization of its own action, as a decision taken once and for all and from which there is no turning back: not the justice of judges, not official justice. *That* kind of justice Francesca mistrusts and despises: that kind of justice is a part of the injustice that there is in things.

"After my son was dead," began Francesca, "the magistrate came to make his report, and he seemed angry. 'Don't take any notice of all those workmen looking at you,' I said. 'All you have to do is your ordinary legal duty; we won't say you're doing it out of affection because he was human flesh and blood like you. *You* feel yourself to be an exalted kind of person, and *this person here* didn't seem of any importance to you at all.' Then he gave a contemptuous shake of his head, and said: 'Ah, it wasn't the moment to do it!' When I heard him talking like that, I turned round and said to him: 'Oh you coward, you're quite right to say it wasn't the moment, because you're thinking of the elections and you're losing ground. When you're in power, then, are you going to come in here and kill me? Is that the sort of discipline you bring with you? Why do you make this report just in order to deceive us? Why don't you go home? Certainly, it wasn't the moment.' "

And so, face to face with the injustice that there is in things, stands injustice, which is a certainty. But Francesca's reply is not the anarchic, individualist reply that puts arms into the hand of the brigand and thrusts him forth to exile and ostracism and the woods: it is a political reply, bound up with the idea of a common law that is a power upon which one can rely, a power that is the enemy of power: the Party. The law which gives Francesca certainty is not authority or its instruments: these belong by nature to the enemy world.

She told us of the first peaceful occupation of the land in 1951, the first time her son led the peasants and was then arrested. "We had gone up onto the mountain; there were more than three hundred of us; while we were there, having a bite to eat, some of us sitting down, some walking about, and no one doing any damage, a police sergeant and a constable arrived from Sciara, and he said: 'Please, please, please put away your flags.' Because we were holding up our flags, unfurled. The peasants said: 'No, why should we take down our flags; what's the reason? The flags aren't doing any harm. And we're not doing any damage here.' But the police sergeant said: 'Let's go to the village, then; let's go to the village.' So off we went to the village. When we were still a little way from it, we saw, down below, the police and the superintendent, and they stopped us: 'Hands up!' We had no guns or explosives or anything. They stopped us and took all our names and Christian names—my son, and Polizzi, and Tirruso, and Ceruti, and Lentini whom we call the mayor of Favara. They asked me my name. He said: 'And you, what are you called?'

" 'My name's in the parish register, if you want to know it.'

" 'Move on, then,' he said. Some of us went one way, some another; there were five or six policemen. One of them said: 'You chose this bad day on purpose. We've got our boots wet and our trousers all covered with earth.'

" 'But for us,' I answered, 'for us today is the most beautiful day in the world, beautiful and quiet and sunny. This is an enjoyment we have never had before. If you don't give us the uncultivated land, according to the law (why should the land go to waste?), you'll have plenty of days like this. This one is only the first.' And so off we went to the village. When we arrived there, they invited my son and four others to go to the town offices as a committee for discussing and getting the facts clear. And my son came home, he changed his clothes in order to go to the town offices, thinking it was the right thing to do, because we had never been taught how to make demonstrations of this kind. While they were in the office discussing, the police arrived with a truck; they put them on the truck and took them away to Termini, to prison."

Law is one thing, authority another. Her son, she says, wished to make them respect the law, the sixty and forty per cent, the eight-hour day; but the authorities are on the side of those who break the laws. When Salvatore, a few days before his death, first took action for the eight-hour day in the quarry and was challenged by the superintendents, he went and reported the matter to the police sergeant at Sciara, and the police sergeant answered: "It's none of my business," and refused to intervene. Next day there was a strike; the company promised to respect the eight-hour day and to pay the arrears of wages. Francesca related how, while they were at work, the superintendent of police from Termini arrived, accompanied by Antonino Mangiafridda, who was overseer of the princess' trucks.

"The superintendent sent for Carnevale, my son, out of the whole lot. 'Carnevale, come here. Now mind what I say, you're the poison of the workers.' While my son was answering him and saying he was not the poison of the workers, but was merely defending the law, Mangiafridda turned round and said to him: 'That's enough of that gangster talk. You won't last long if you try that kind of insolence.'

"The superintendent did not take any action against Mangiafridda. If it had been my son who had spoken those words, the superintendent would have arrested him and taken him away, but as it was Mangiafridda who said them—it's he who is the criminal, the evildoer of Sciara, he who was the princess' warehouseman—he did not arrest *him*, and they went away. That was the thirteenth, Friday."

Francesca's endless discourse was thick with such episodes, at every moment, and with similar contemptuous criticisms of the authorities. She is brimful of hostility and violence; she has made a complete break, with no half-measures, a break that is founded upon an unshakable certainty. She has broken away from an age-old situation, from the passive recognition that against this kind of reality there is nothing to be done. Without this certainty nothing would be possible except despair, and such a break

194

would be unthinkable except in the poetical form of a funeral lament, or by an escape into mythology, by faith in another world, by identification of the dead man with Christ. For her, too, her son is Christ, but in a perfectly realistic way (as for instance, with the police sergeant who, like Pilate, said: "It's none of my business"); in a way that is firmly tied to earth and which demands, not love, but justice. Hence this cold passion, this impulse toward action, this *élan*, which has something of the same nature as the urge which moved the Jewish peasants of San Nicandro Garganico to emigrate, by different ways and with a different destiny, in search of justice on this earth. But the earth, for Francesca, is not elsewhere; it is here, at Sciara, in Sicily, and war is waged with words, here in the tribunal of this room.

"Who kills me kills Jesus Christ," Salvatore had said to the Mafia man who had been sent to threaten him five or six days before his death. "It was night, and my son was coming back from work, when from a dark corner he heard himself called, in a whisper: 'Pss, pss.' He did not turn and he did not answer. Then the man appeared out of the shadow and came up to him. He clapped a hand on his shoulder. 'Oh, Totò,' he said, 'you're getting very proud.' 'I have a name that God gave me.'

" 'Well, well,' the man went on, 'I like you; if I didn't like you I wouldn't get mixed up in these troubles. What you've got to do is to get out of the Party and tear up all the papers and forget about the whole thing. You'll get a good sum of money, so

195

that as long as you live you won't have to work any more.'

" 'I'm not to be bought and sold,' said my son, 'and I'm not an opportunist.'

" 'You'd better think it over; otherwise you'll come to a bad end.'

"And then Salvatore answered: 'Come and kill me then, but tell those who sent you that when they've killed me they've killed Jesus Christ.'

"When my son arrived home he was agitated, and while he was eating his supper, here at this table, he kept striking himself on the head, like this, with his two hands, but he did not speak, all he said was: 'They won't convince me.' But he was pale as a corpse. All he took was just two spoonfuls of spaghetti and then he stopped eating. 'Won't you tell your mother what's happened?' He wouldn't. But afterward he told me. But he did not tell me the name of the man. He told me he would say it in public, at the meeting, on Sunday. But on Sunday the meeting couldn't be held because it was forbidden, because of the feast of the patron saint; and on Monday, at dawn, they killed him."

"Who kills me kills Jesus Christ," repeated Francesca. But she knows that her church is still in full vigor ("if a monk dies they don't close the monastery"). And this power, this earthly church that keeps her alive, that has wiped away her tears, that has loosened her tongue, has also given her a language. It is not the poetical language of the Lucanian mother recounting the life of her dead son: it is a language of vindication, of oratory, of discussion, an act of accusation—a Party language. Its very terms sound new and strange in dialect—legal and political terms, law and reform, the sixty and forty per cent, the struggle, the organization, the opportunists, and so on. But in her mouth, in face of death, this language, this conventional, monotonous Party language becomes a language of heroes, being, indeed, the first vehicle for asserting one's own existence, the arid chant of a new fury on the first day of its existence in a new world. This new existence has come to birth in the form of tragedy; it is obscure, detailed, difficult to understand, fierce. It is a revelation, both in the tribunal of the consciousness, and in the real tribunal at Palermo; a moment of truth attained, which gives life and motion to all things and which is repeated unwearyingly, in a narration now fixed and never again to be lost, just as the certainty attained is never to be lost either. The death of her son has opened her eyes, has made of her a new and different person, supremely strong, indifferent to others, superior to all things because sure of this new existence upon which she has entered. Before, she was a woman like any other, a poor peasant woman, a stranger here at Sciara, for she came from a village in the Messina province, deserted by her husband, who disappeared and then died. She came here with this son of hers when he was five months old, unwelcome, perhaps, at first, because she was a stranger and alone.

"I went out to work so as to earn enough to keep

my little son, then he grew and went to school, but he was still very small, so I did all sorts of jobs in order to earn money for him. I went olive picking; when the olives were finished the peas began, when the peas were finished the almonds began, when the almonds were finished the olives began again, and then cutting grass, grass to make forage for the animals and corn to use for ourselves, and I had to dig too because there was the child and I didn't want *him* to suffer, and I didn't want anyone to look down upon him, even in my own family. I had to work all day long and I left the child with my sister. Father he had none, so my brother-in-law took him for some years to train him for work in the fields. I sent him to school till he reached the fifth grade; he had his diploma and he went every day, and then we did our best to earn a living until he went to do his military service."

So Salvatore had grown up without a father, and even as a child had had to experience a special situation even more difficult than that of other peasant children; and he had grown up full of pride. He had made two attempts to escape from his restricted world: he had been a candidate for entry into the police, but had not been accepted because of an uncle's penal record, and had also applied to become a military driver; in this he was unsuccessful because, owing to a delay in the preparation of documents, he was found to have passed the age limit. He was not one to accept a state of servility, but the peasant movement saved him from individual protest, from the revolt of the bandit; and he became a union organizer. But in this his mother, still tied to the old customs, could not follow him.

"At the time when the first elections took place," Francesca told us, "there was still no Party here at Sciara, and Salvatore said to me: 'Mother, I want you to vote for Garibaldi. You can't mistake him, he's the one with a cap on, you'll recognize him, don't forget.'

"'No, I won't forget.' He made me promise. But when I went to vote and saw God's blessed Cross, I said to myself: 'This is the God I know. How can I betray Him for one I don't know?' And I put my mark against the Cross. I said nothing about it to him: but the votes for Garibaldi, in the whole village, were only just seven, and it wasn't worth while. Salvatore was furious. He was always a bit nervous; and he became like a Lucifer. But I never told him anything about how I had voted. Then, when the Party was formed here at Sciara, the day he signed his name and took charge of it as secretary, I cried all the evening. 'My son,' I said, 'you're stabbing me to the heart; don't put yourself at the head of it. Vote for it, yes, but don't put yourself at the head of it; you know Sciara is an unlucky place, it's nothing but a handful of criminals, and you know you've got no father and we have to work for our living.' But he answered that they were all friends together and that I mustn't be afraid. I didn't want to be; but I was the mother of a Socialist now, and what was I to do?"

199

Thus began the young peasant's political work, founded upon the feeling of a new law and of the free examination of that law; there began also, at the same time, his struggle against the Mafia, against its oft-repeated flatteries and threats. But his mother, at that time, had not yet become what she is today; she had not yet broken free of ancient customs and ancient fears. His aunt—who came into the house at this point—has still remained to a great extent what she was before. She sat down near us and did not speak, but I could see that she could not escape from the old thought that the blame of her nephew's death lay in his political activity. She is younger than her sister, and her face is more human, her eyes more moist with feeling. She too had been a mother to the little boy, whom she had brought up while her sister was working in the fields; and, when you look at her, she seems, in her heartbroken silence, to be related to the dead man in a more deep-seated physical way, and to be more defenseless, like a wounded animal. But Francesca did not interrupt the tale she was now telling of her son's childhood, of his first struggles, of the two years he spent at Montevarchi ("Cursed be the day when I asked him to come back!"), of his gestures, of his replies to officials, of his work among his peasant companions. When she told of her son's sayings, of his great and noble phrases (as, for instance, when a police officer pointed a pistol at him on his return on horseback, flag in hand, from a land occupation ceremony, and he said to him: "Shoot! I am here simply for the honor of the people"; and many others too), she did not distort the truth, out of theatrical feeling, but seemed to be aware of it for the first time, and this sufficed to give the phrases nobility and grandeur. Her discourse is a gospel, a humble, detective story gospel of truth, a testimony of the truth. This is all that counts for her. While she was speaking came the sound of the bell from the church nearby. She did not break off, but I saw her rapidly make the sign of the cross and heard her murmur: "Holy bell, witness of truth."

Warnings of death, offers, threats—Salvatore had many of them; and the tale of each one of them was long, circumstantial, precise, documented, going back to those at the beginning and at the time when he was in prison at Termini, and Tardibuono came to his mother and said: "Where's he getting to, with this Party? All that happens is, they put him behind bars and others gather the olives. It's a party of cads and brawlers. If he gets out of it, we'll give him the best bit of land, and the olives . . ." The most recent threats were those of the man who spoke to him in the dark, on the 10th or 11th of May, and those of Mangiafridda, on the 13th. On Sunday he was unable to hold the meeting at which he was intending to give the names of the men who were going to kill him. That evening there was a *festa* in the court-yard of the princess' castle, and they were waiting for him there: but he, as it were by presentiment, refused to go; instead, he went to the cinema with his mother and aunt.

"He was rather worried at not having had the meeting; and then they went and gave a very unlucky film. There was a husband, and a wife, and another man with an ax, and they hit him over the head with the ax and cut his head off. My son said: 'Look how they kill their enemies'; and then he got up with a face like death and said to me: 'I'm going to bed, you stay here.' When the cinema ended, about one o'clock, I came home with my chair and found my son in bed, reading. He used to sleep here, and I slept up in the loft. He always studied in bed at night, every evening for two or three hours, till very late. That night I had a dream, I dreamed I was singing; oh, what a lovely voice I had, and what applause! But a song at night is tears in the morning. Next day I had to go to work. At half past five I left him combing his hair and went out to the haystack. When I came back, my son was going away along the road. I had to go out into the fields, but it was still early and I started making the bread. I was making bread when my son died.

"While I was making the bread my brother-in-law arrived: there was already a rumor in the village that somebody had been killed, but I knew nothing about it. He asked me if Totò had gone to the quarry, at what time he had started, and if he was alone. His face was pale and I grew suspicious. I thought of a possible misfortune, and I started crying. He told me somebody had been killed, but it was an old man, and he was going to find out about it. I ran about the village asking for news; I saw

202

people crying, but no one would tell me anything. So I started out along the road my son had taken, and with me was a woman whose husband was at the quarry. I hurried quickly along, looking to see whether my brother-in-law and my brother were coming back; if they came back, it was not my son, but if they did not come back, then it was. While I was on the road, I heard the sound of a car. It came round the bend, and I saw it was Mangiafridda. I stopped him and said: 'Tell me the truth, who is it who's dead?'

" 'From the position he's lying in you can't tell,' said Mangiafridda. 'The police sergeant and other policemen are there and they won't let anyone go near. Truly, on the honor of my mother, they wouldn't let me see.'

"When he said to me: 'The police sergeant and other policemen are there'—they who were closer than brothers to him, they were always together, they used to eat together when they were working in the fields, when they were threshing together with the princess' men—then I said to him: 'The police sergeant didn't tell *you* who the dead man was? *You?*'

"My nerves were so upset that it seemed to me I was walking in some kind of a machine, and not on foot, and so I went on; and the woman who was with me kept running up and catching me by the arm. 'Let go of me and let me get on, please let me go.' So at last I came to where the dead man was. But who was I? I was like lightning, I moved like someone in desperation, my feet no longer touched the ground.

203

When I arrived, my brother-in-law was the first to come to me: 'Don't run,' he said, 'because it's not your son.' But his face was the face of a dead man. When I took a step forward, the police sergeant from Sciara came up to me: 'Signora, it's not your son.' While they were telling me it was not my son, I took another step forward and I saw the feet of the dead man, who was lying face downward and all covered over, and only his feet were sticking out, but I saw his white socks: they were the socks I had washed the day before for my son, which he had put on that morning, and the feet were placed just as my son used to place his feet, like this. They would not let me go close. The superintendent of police from Termini came to me. 'If you have sons and are a Christian,' I said to him (the superintendent began to cry), 'you must take me to my son; these cowards say he's not my son, but he is my son.' 'You know he may not be touched,' he said. 'I won't touch him, I only want to see him: he is my son, in his legs he is my son, in his feet he is my son, in the way he lies he is my son, I want to see his face.' Three times I pushed forward so as to be able to see his face: but it was hidden. The policemen had placed themselves on each side of me and they were holding me and watching me.

" 'When they came and killed my son no one came and watched, and now they are watching me,' I said. 'I haven't killed anyone, I who brought him up for thirty-two years, and now because I want to go and see him you are watching me. You watch *me*, but those others, you let them go free.' And then, turning my back, I said: 'My son, and how did they kill you, and did they place you like that, in that nice, tidy way?' On the ground there was no mark, nothing at all; when a man's shot, when he's killed, surely he must make some kind of movement, either he lies with his neck twisted, or his arms thrown out, or with one leg stretched out . . . surely he doesn't lie just as he falls. Until his blood is cold he must make some kind of movement. There must be a spasm, a convulsion as he lies on the ground. But here, there was nothing; it looked as if he had gone to bed in the evening, he was lying in such a nice, tidy way, face downward so that you couldn't look into his face, but fine and straight as a candle. Three times I pushed forward to try and see his face.

"They took me away from beside my son and sent me home. I was sitting on a stone; first I sat on a stone up above and then, since I could not see him from there, I sat at the side, and I cried. Then the police came and tried to make me tell them whether he had any enemies because of women or money, but they knew quite well who it was that had made him die. Then in the evening they took him from the cemetery and brought him to me here in the house, they took him into the church and we gave him the holy water, they gave him all the funeral rites they could, they brought him to the village and then to the municipal offices. Four men they arrested, but they will have to catch the ones who sent them, as well. I see him all the time in front of my eyes; I don't remember now how he came into the house, how he walked, I only remember him lying on the ground, face downward on the path."

A number of peasants had come, one by one, into the room, old men and young men with eyes that shone like glowing coal; they stood against the wall and listened in silence to this gospel narrative. But it was late in the evening by this time, and we had to leave. I went down the steps outside the door, and up the dark street. Here and there on the ground great black masses, like scattered rocks in a meadow, made the darkness yet darker. These were cows, the big, dark Sciara cows, lying asleep on the road: when my eyes became accustomed to the night they looked to me like black statues of archaic beasts in some imaginary China. Farther on, a white patch lay motionless on the ground, and I saw it was a dog; but it was not asleep, it was dead.

At the top of the steps leading up to the main street, in the feeble light of an electric lamp with a flat white shade—like an ordinary lamp in a room— some young *contadini* were waiting for me. They spoke of Salvatore—so honest, so wholehearted in the workers' cause, so clean, such a hard worker; and they insisted on my going with them to the Labor Exchange. It is an ordinary peasant house, a room giving onto the street, all hung with manifestoes. Hens were asleep in one corner. It is the home of the secretary, a dried-up old peasant; and the family dinner table is the office table too. There were peasants sitting all round, talking like conspirators. You can see from their faces which are the violent ones and which the diffident, and you can see exemplified all the different ways of behavior in this world that is on the move, this world in which they feel themselves, obscurely, to be protagonists—but in an extremely difficult sort of way; for they are wrapped round in a tangle of ancient bonds and ancient terrors which this recent death might have been expected to fasten yet tighter, but which, unexpectedly, it has severed. The most lively person there was a little boy, the secretary's son, active, gay, enthusiastic, proud of being a fearless hawk, the only red hawk* among all the yellow hawks of the Sciara feudal estate. When I went out into the street again, they all came to the door and bade me farewell— "Comrade, comrade." In their mouths it is a magic word, a formula of conspiracy which gives strength and power, and which suffices, like the trumpets in the Bible, to make the walls of the city fall down flat.

I wanted to walk about the streets for a little, but it was difficult to be alone. A young peasant went with me. He used to study with Salvatore in the evenings, he told me. They were studying the vocabulary. There the words were, the words they have discovered and which only now have become necessary. He insisted on paying for a cup of coffee for me, and there was nothing I could do to avoid this—not wishing to hurt his feelings—when he pulled some precious little coins out of his pocket. I

* The "Red Hawks" are a Socialist youth organization.

left him in the piazza and went up again, by myself, toward the castle, circling round the sleeping cows. A sleeping she goat was reclining against a doorpost with the languid weariness of a woman, its hoofs lying limply abandoned. In the darkness below the castle two invisible people were playing mouth organs, answering each other from a distance. A field guard went by on horseback: the clip-clop of his horse's hoofs resounded on the stone paving. Against the star-filled sky rose the outline of Monte San Calogero; a single electric lamp lit up the sloping sides of little one-story houses, the last houses in the village, with the emptiness of the open country beyond. The sky seemed immense; vague mists were rising from the sea and resting upon the village, upon the sleeping cows, upon the turnip plants in the fields. I walked down again toward the car. In the darkness I heard the clamor of a quarrel, and someone leaning against a wall said to me: *"Lite tra padre e figlio, non ci vuole consiglio."* (A quarrel between father and son, no advice wanted.) People were closing their doors and putting out the fires on the hearths, sleep was coming down upon Sciara, and we went off into the night.

During the following days I went back many times to the house in Sciara. Something drew me to the place, as it were into a black whirlpool, and there, each time, was the village again, and the evil peacefulness of the castle, and the church with the tombs of the Notarbartolo family, princes of Sciara and of

208

Castelreale, gentlemen-in-waiting; and the bare room with the small bed at the far end, and on its white walls the Madonna of Altavilla, Santa Rita, Jesus, the Holy Family and the *Worker's Almanac;* and the woman who moved her black veil with her hands as she talked; and the somber, ceaseless voice speaking as though it would never stop until the day of judgment.

The last time I went, I took the Caccamo road from Termini; I was being driven by a new chauffeur, a young man with a thin mustache and the respectful manners of a clerk. The road rises up from the coast between slopes oozing with olive oil; then one comes in among the mountains and the eye roams over the blue expanses of the feudal estates, and the Castle of Caccamo stands up, solemn and enormous, upon its rock. Caccamo, like Sciara, lies between castle and church, in the midst of cornfields; but it is not, like Sciara, a mere village; it spreads out and covers the whole of the mountainside. We stopped and looked at it from the main road, a compact, solid body of a thousand houses, with the shape of a great bird or a dove with folded wings lying upon the mountain. The sky suddenly darkened, and before we started off again the first drops of rain were falling. It was a summer storm, swift and fierce, and the new road to Sciara, upon which Salvatore had worked, was already a torrent, and lightning was flashing on the slopes of San Calogero, and a mist of water dimmed the distant outlines of the Cerda mountains. Some field guards caught in the storm passed by on horseback, covered up in waterproof sheets; the stubble in the fields was smoking. Then, as suddenly as it had come, the tempest ceased, and, driving through pools and streams, we came down into the piazza at Sciara. Francesca, sitting beside the bed, greeted me once more and gave me a post card, a portrait of her son as a boy of sixteen, dressed in his best Sunday clothes, with a big American tie; the round, boyish face, its black eyes full of determination and fire, resembled slightly, perhaps, the pictures of Giuliano as a youth, but had a sort of rectitude, of modest pride in its straightforward glance, as of one who intends to be the master of his own destiny. When she said good-by to me, his mother asked me, in her assured, imperious way, to write the "romance" of her son's death. She embraced me, and I left her sitting on her chair alone, with her voice, her dry, even, somber voice that never stops.

Once again we drove along the warm coast toward Palermo. The driver told me about himself and his life. He had been a policeman at the time of the repressions; and it had been a hard life, a useless sacrifice. Now he was earning twenty-nine thousand lire a month; he had a wife and a little girl, and fortunately they could live with his mother and thus avoid paying any rent. Politics did not interest him: no party, according to him, was satisfactory. Nevertheless, with some hesitation—for he did not know what I myself thought about it—he confessed to me that he had had, in the past, some sympathy with the

M.S.I.* Because, he said, it was a "social" party. Something social is needed, he said, because people can't go on with the sort of poverty there is at present; but this party had failed, and so in the last elections he had abandoned it and had considered voting for the Socialists. The only way to solve the problem of living was the social way, the way of Socialism. How could one manage to live? In point of fact he believed, also, in another way. He had a passion for gambling, for any kind of gambling, but particularly racing. "I put everything I can save on horses, and one of these days I'm bound to win. A lady said to me: 'With the thousand lire you put on horses, you could buy some jam for your little girl.' I know that, but jam is always jam, and horses might turn into meat, beefsteaks, a house, everything we need." Thus his hopes were founded upon either justice or fortune and he had not made his choice between the two—the only two methods, mythologically speaking, for enduring extreme poverty.

Palermo welcomed me again that evening, like a great ant heap, highly colored, dramatic, full of splendor and desire. There sits the town, facing the sea, beset by the mountains and the feudal estates, and round it are the bandits in their desert haunts, the fishermen of Trappeto, the men shut up in cages at Partinico, the labyrinthine structure of the Mafia, the brigand with his desperate, individual protest, answered by the personal initiative of men like Dolci and, on the other hand, by the somber mother of

* *Movimiento Sociale Italiano,* the neo-fascist party.

Sciara, with her accusations, her Party, the peasant movement.

On the quay, when the steamer left for Naples, a large crowd collected, and there were good-bys and waving handkerchiefs, for this was a real separation, a real abandonment. Night enfolded us at sea and went with us all the way to Naples, where the first dawn greeted us, clear and blue. Disembarking at Naples we passed through a customhouse as though landing in another country. The city, in the early light, opened out all white and gray before us and seemed full of a nervous tenderness, its streets already busy with different trades and with men intent, in an ancient harmony, each upon his unknown fate. Sicily was far away. And now, in the luminous morning, the train bore me away to Rome, Rome that is both too conscious and too ignorant, asleep in her limitless history and in the torpor of a hot summer day.